BOSNIA AND THE SREBRENICA TRAGEDY

Before and after 1995

Courtesy of UNHCR.

BOSNIA AND THE SREBRENICA TRAGEDY

Before and after 1995

Luckshan Abeysuriya

ISBN
0-9531839-3-9

Published by
Luckshan Abeysuriya MA, PGCE

Printed by MTP Media, The Sidings, Beezon Fields, Kendal, Cumbria LA9 6BL

CONTENTS

I dedicate this book to all the people of Bosnia and to my parents. Pictured above are my beloved late parents Dr Fred Abeysuriya MRCP (Edinburgh 1917) and Mrs Beatrice Abeysuriya shown at their silver wedding in 1951. I am indebted to my parents for my education and support of my early career.

▲ *Our four children, Maya, Rohan, Suranee and Nina.*

◀ *Barbara on our Wedding Day, 4/4/64.*

Foreword

In the spring of 1974 I spent six weeks in Melbourne, Australia as a Winston Churchill Fellow. While I was there I spent a considerable amount of time alongside Yugoslavians who were working at the Colt car factory. One night the Yugoslavian Muslim guest workers and I were watching the FA Cup Final on television together. During the interval they told me how there were working long hours and sending home their money so that when their three-year contracts ended and they returned to their own country they would be able to build new homes for their wives and families with the money they had accrued.

Since retiring as a Methodist minister and coming to live in Morecambe, I became a good friend of Luckshan Abeysuriya through the South Lakeland and Lancaster City Branch of the United Nations Association. Until recently Luckshan was the Branch Secretary.

I was filled with admiration when I heard that he was travelling to Bosnia to see for himself the siutation in which the Bosnian Muslims now find themselves. We are about the same age but because I have acute diabetes, unlike him, I am housebound.

For these reasons I have great pleasure in writing this Foreword. I do not claim to be a politican, economist or lawyer so I cannot judge the strength of his agruments versus those who would wish to stress a different point of view about the Slav peoples. As a highly qualified sociologist and fieldworker my approach has been from the humanistic point of view of the sociology of religion as Berger put it in his book 'Invitation to Sociology' (Pelican, Penguin Books, London, 1963, p7). Therefore I respect Luckshan's right to say the things he has written because I know they come from the heart.

I commend this book to all those who are sufficiently open-minded to explore the current situation in Bosnia from all points of view.

Rev. Terry Walton
Morecambe, United Kingdom.
8 October 2006

Acknowledgements and Thank You

My book would not be possible if not for the generous help, advice and encouragement by many here in UK and Bosnia.

I wish to thank most sincerely the following:- for generous donations for my research trip to Bosnia and Herzegovina, and for the cost of the book.

The Furness Multi-Cultural Community Forum, Barrow-in-Furness. Reverend Terrence and Mavis Walton, Morecambe. John and Ann Harrison, Newcastle-upon-Tyne. Anthony and Denise Close of Hunters Hill Sydney. Frank and Marjorie Crosland, Kendal. Mrs Mary Harrison, Bradford. Malcolm and Ann McCrindle, Kendal. Alf and Kathy Nelson, Kendal. Father Parker, Catholic Church, Grange-over-Sands. Hassan and Sha Sheriff, Hemel Hempstead. HRH Prince Fredrick van Lauenberg, Netherlands.

I thank profusely my friend Lord Robin Corbett of Castle Vale for his kind advice, help and contacts, also to Lord Anderson of Swansea and Lord Hannay of Cheswick for their expertise. To Dr. Nina Caspersen PhD and Professor Christopher May of Department of International Relations, Lancaster University for their kind academic guidance.

To Martin Bell for his advice and help. Also to Mr Mansur Jusic of the Bosnian Embassy in London and Foreign Ministry Sarajevo and Paul Dudman of London-Dockland Campus for his kind help and giving me valuable material from UNHCR achives on the Srebrenica and Bosnian war.

To staff of the Quaker Peace and Social Witness in UK and former Yugoslavia. To Jane Sharpe, Manager of Workbase, Kendal and to Matthew O'Connor there, for their patient and diligent work in converting my hand written manuscript into Word for the printers.

To Mike Miller MD, and Gary Craig at MTP Media Solutions at Kendal for printing my book, designing an excellent cover and good turn-around.

To Jim Robinson and his staff of Airlink Taxis Haysham for care and transport to and from Grange to Manchester airport for my visits to Sarajevo.

In Bosnia and Herzegovina, in both Serajevo and Srebrenica, I made several friends whose help and camaraderie is most appreciated. I enjoyed my 14 day stay there with help from many.

Bentbasa (old city) Bascaraji, and the Unity and Brotherhood Bridge were some of my treasured "haunts" in Sarajevo.

I must thank the following friends in Bosnia and Herzegovina, both for kindness and advice before and after my visit there. Aisa Telalovic, Information Manager British Council, Sarajevo. Majda Priljac, External Relations Officer,

UNHCR, Sarajevo. Asja Ascengic of UNDP. Press staff at OSCE and OHR and valuable web-information. Lt Commander Karen Halsley of EUFOR for advice on the security situation there.

To the wonderful young staff of Emona Hotel, BentBaša, to Nejla (Manager), Edina, Senita, Adnan and Farid, who made my ten day stay there home from home.

To Mirza, the strong bell boy of Holiday Inn Hotel where I stayed the first three nights, and his friend Amar, the taxi driver who safely drove me to Srebrencia, Potocari and Bruntanac and back to Sarajevo and acted as my guide there.

I owe a debt of gratitude to Shaba and Sauda, two brave mothers and wives of Srebrenica and Zepa enclaves victims. They gave me graphic and touching information on the tragedy and on their brave work to find the many remains of their loved ones. They also gave me valuable post-cards and a graphic tee-shirt "Do not forget Genocide in Srebrenica" displayed in my book.

Also I must thank several young and old people who willingly talked to me about the Sarajevo siege and tragedy of 1995, especially to two people – Melissa Dizdavevic a very bright Sarajevo university student who wishes to come to Cambridge and to Mr and Mrs Kavahasonvic of Photo-Shop Bascaraji, the latter who patiently processed 150 digital shots I took in Bosnia and Herzegovina, and displayed in this book.

Back in the UK, John Harrison my nephew in Newcastle and to Jim Byrne of Grange both historians for proof reading and advising on editorial matters. Also to Dr Tony Akbar, Barrow, for his friendly advice on publishing.

I must thank my wife Barbara and family for their support, and for kindly compiling the index, and for sustaining me during this arduous task; to all of them mentioned, I am in debt, including my loveable cat Sampras who was a great comfort.

Lord Corbett merits special thanks again for hosting the book launch at the House of Lords, Westminster on 5th December and for his generosity and kindness, and to Rev. Terrence and Mavis Walton for writing an excellent Foreword to my book at short notice.

I hope to re-visit Sarajevo in January 2007 to launch the book there with help from friends in Bosnia Herzegovina

The culture of Turkish Coffee, à la Bosnia.

The hotel at BentBaša, Sarajevo, where the author was accommodated.

My cat Sampras enjoying the Sarajevo rug.

Chapter One

Introducton and Preface

I have decided to write a book on the Srebrenica tragedy of 1995, and in Bosnia, its initial causes, its consequences and aftermath for three reasons. First I met Marshall Tito in 1957 in Sri Lanka. Secondly as a Human Rights activist I wish to help the survivors of Srebrenica to seek peace and justice. Finally as a UN-Man, I wish to know why the UN failed in the early days, and how its subsequent success over there came about.

On the 11th of July, 1995, in the UN safe haven of Srebrenica in the Eastern Bosnian borders with Serbia, the worst atrocity since World War 2 happened. More than 7,100 Mulim-Bosnia men and boys were executed by overwhelmingly superior Bosnian-Serb forces under the command of General Rakto Mladic. This wanton destruction of the lives of many thousands of innocent civilians who were rounded up in the town, is called by Richard Holbrooke[1], an US Under-Secretary of the Clinton Administration, being as horrific in the annals of modern war as Lidice, Oradour, Babi-Yar and Katyn Forest.

The superior Serb forces held 340 Ductch UN peace-keepers of UNPROFOR "captive" while the horror was perpetrated over the next four days. The ICRC have recorded the deaths of 7,179 males, most of the victims were unarmed civilians and many died in ambushes, and mass executions that followed in the town of Zvornik where the Serb-Bosnian forces rounded up the victims prior to the gruesome executions by shooting them at close range. In Richard Holbrooke's[2] seminal book "On how to win a War" he says "for sheer intensity nothing in the Bosnia-Serb War of 1992-5 had matched or would match Srebrenica".

The world was shocked, the UN and EU felt they had to act. The Western Alliance was greatly affected by this grave human rights violation of genocide and mass ethnic cleansing. Not only Srebrenica, but Zepa and Gorazde which were UN safe areas were affected, but in Bihac in the west, Muslim-Bosnian forces with UN/NATO help were able to mitigate the Serb-Bosnian aggression after the Croats spectacular advances in adjoining Krajina.

Inevitably such questions as the following presented themselves:-

- *Why did Srebrenica happen?*
- *Why did the International Community let it happen?*
- *Could have NATO and UN prevented the massacre?*
- *Could a similar event take place again in the 21st Century?*
- *All these questions, are addressed in my book.*

Srebrenica was not just a only horror story of the war, but it was planned and executed by the brutal cruelty of the actors there. At the same place and in the same area it led to mass rape of Muslim women and young girls. Mass rape as a manifestation of war is now a war crime, this is underpinned by International Law as a crime against Humanity. All three combatants - Croats, Serbs and Bosniaks in the three Balkans War are alleged to have perpetrated this inhuman action.

My book will run into 13 chapters, with chapter 2 an interesting history of Bosnia-Herzegovina from the 6th century Slavic invasion, the Ottoman period which influenced the whole Balkans immensely, followed by the Austro-Hungarian Empire; the First World War Yugoslavia; Titoism and then the Second World War and the post Cold-War and final distintegration of Yugoslavia; and the rapid emergance of Nationalism and Regionalism up to the 21st Century. In chapter 3, I shall draw upon my knowledge of Marshall Tito's Socialism and his ability untill the 1980s to keep the six Republics of Former Socialist Yugoslavia under central control. Chapter 4 will focus on the fall of Communism and the collapse of the former Soviet Union and its impact on the Balkans. Also I will look at the emergance of ultra nationalism and regional politicians in the Balkans and their aspirations for a Greater Serbia.

Chapter 5 will deal with the early involvement of the UN with the Security Council's arms embargo on former Yugoslavia, the work of UNPROFOR, its early set-backs and successes and also the yeomen services of UNHCR which had to deal with near two million refugees and internally displaced persons. Chapter 6 looks at how the UN-Safe areas concept were policed and serviced in the midst of greater odds with a limited mandate and lack of adequate resources and manpower. How far did the UN arms embargo work or not?

Chapter 7 is part of the heart of the book, about the long and most damaging Siege of Sarajevo by Serb forces, who encircled the city from the surrounding mountains, its daily bombardment, cruel damage and attrition of the old, young and brave Sarajevans who were lacking in food, water, gas and electricity. I shall look at the good work of UNPROFOR and UNCHR, in airlifting essential supplies to the city and dealing with the vast amount of IDPs. Chapters 8 and 9 are about the tragic details on Srebrenica, its location, its people and eventual massacres. What can one learn from such behaviour in war and the ethnic hatred and damage it did to iner-communal harmony? What can we learn from it to help prevent such ethnic cleansing, rape and genocide elsewhere? In this chapter I hope to share with my readers the vivid and important field research and meetings of the communities there and case studies upon my visit in July 2006.

Sarajevo funerals, 1992-3.

In chapter 10 we shall look at the establishment in late 1993 by the UNSC of the ICTFY, its success and failure to meet out justice on the indictment of War Criminals. Was the trial of late Slobadan Milosevic too long and the evidence too weak. The indictment, arrest, punishment of the two Serb-Bosnians Mladic and Karadzic. (Why are they not in the dock? at present – Oct-06). I shall in this chapter also try to give you a non-legal summary on the prospects for a very important case in the ICJ where for the first time a State (Bosnia) has filed action against another sovereign State (Serbia) for the crime of genocide. The first hearing was held in February 2006, and already legal commentators feel it may take five to six years for the ICJ to arrive at a final judgement.

Chaper 11 will be a detailed analysis of the Dayton Peace Accords and its Institutional Frameworks agreed in Paris on December 1995 to end the Balkans Wars. How and why did the western alliance commit over 60,000 NATO troops including 20,000 US personnel, after the Srebrenica tragedy to end the Wars of 1991-5: why the diplomatic trade-offs and lengthy negotiations by Richard Holbrooke and others. What are Dayton's strengths and weakness in hind-sight? What are its strains and multi-ethnic relations in Bosnia now. Chapter 12 will look to the future, to the hopes, aspirations and expectations of the three Countries who were engaged in the Balkans wars, to accede to the wider European Union.

Could Croatia, Serbia and Bosnia-Herzegovina, engage in accession talks with a view to joining the Union? The author will draw upon his wide knowledge of the European Commission and Union and give you an expert evaluation on the prospects for accession by the these countries. What are the important criteria to be met and what pitfalls lie ahead before this dream is realised by the three communities who are aware of the immense benefits of membership not only of the EU but also NATO. The EU/OSCE and NATO still need to work hard to help these three emerging democracies along the way to Brussels.

Chapter 13 is the final chapter, conclusion and epilogue of the book, where I shall draw together all the different strands from the history of Bosnia to the near future (General Elections in October 2006) to evaluate the options for peace and prosperity in the Western Balkans.

This book is a partial dedication to the brave survivors of the four year conflict in the Balkans and to the revered memory of those who perished. It is my legacy to a better understanding of human rights and more harmonious empathy of Inter-Communal relations in the Balkans and elsewhere. I would request you humbly to read this book (a labour of love for peace and ethnic harmony) and I recommend it to your friends and family.

Luckshan Abeysuriya
October 2006, Grange over Sands
United Kingdom

Chapter Two

History of
Bosnia and Herzegovina
– 6th to 21st Century

Bosnia was the most powerful state in the Balkans region in the Middle Ages[1]. Its name dates back to Roman days. Plentiful supplies of water with its lush rivers, streams and springs perhaps gave its name Bosana (water). Herzegovina was named after the last Duke of Hum, Herceg Stzepan who was the last ruler of the Bosnian aristocrat family Kosaca before the Ottoman Turks invasion in 1483. Bosnia and Herzegovina is not only at the heart of the former Yugoslavia, but also of the Dinaric Alps, which dominate its geography. Bosnia is the Central and northern region of the country and Herzegovina is the southern part of Yugoslavia.

In the 1990 census its total population before the Balkans ructions of 1991-95 was about four million. Bosnia and Herzegovina's place in history has been often overlooked due to its geographical and sometimes cultural isolation from mainstream Europe. The territory of Bosnia and Herezegovinia is scattered with remnants of pre-historic life, human life predating ancient history spanning from the Palaeolithic period to the Illyrian clans. The first millennium in Bosnia saw the process of stabilisation of a broad ethnic and cultural foundation[2] from these tribes belonging to the Iron Age, a culture emerged in ethnic grouping which is called the Illyrians.

The Greeks and the Celtic migrations affected the Illyrians in the Balkans. These influences had a big cultural and spiritual impact and directly led to the greater influence of the Romans. The Romans in 229 BC, crushing the Illyrian navy established a foothold in the Balkans. It was only in 35 BC under Emperor Octavian that the Roman army annexed the Dalmatian coastline. There are still a few historical sites of Illyrian heritage in Bosnia and Herezegovinia left in Vranduk in Central Bosnia, and in Blagaj near the Buna River in Herzegovina archaeological finds have revealed that the culture of antiquity came before the Romans[3].

Now in Bosnia archaeologists and geologists in 2006, seem to have found the remains of a great European pryamid in Visoko near the outskirts of Sarajevo (see photos in book), claiming to be taller than the great pyramid of Giza in Egypt[4]. Some historians claim that Visoko was the medieval capital of Bosnia with a fortress used by Bosnian kings on the top of Visocika hill. Mr Osmanagic, the Bosnia archaeologist, says the fortress was burnt in the 16th century by the invading Turks. The fortress being built on the old Roman observation post, which was in turn constructed on the ruins of an ancient settlement.

Visoko Pyramid, Bosnia Herzegovina, being excavated in the Sarajevo district.

Illyrian culture is largely a mystery but its spiritual and cultural impact has lasted almost two millennia after its demise. With the disappearance of the Illyrians. Bosnia and Herezegovinia became part of the vast Roman empire. The Romans built roads and used Bosnian ore and its lead for the Roman Armies. They also recruited Illyrians to the Imperial legions, providing cheap labour for the Roman adminstration.

Christianity was introduced and largely accepted but elementary Illyrian paganism was maintained and passed on to the Romans. After the slow decline of the Roman empire Bosnia and Herezegovinia suffered new attacks from the Slavs and Avars which occurred in Central and Eastern Balkans, there was seismic social change, leading to a "melange of Cultures"[5] which made their mark on present day Bosnia and Herezegovinia. The Slavs dominated Bosnia from the 6th century AD, and sizeable Slav migrations came from the East. The Avars gradually retreated, but the Slavs remained in their new homeland giving present day Bosnia a very large Serb ethnic group. The Slav influence was marked from about the 10th century. Bosnia was not a vassal state, it remained independent. Assimilation of Slavic values and moves with indigenous Bosnian peoples came much quicker due to its geographic isolation and intervention.

In the coastal areas Slavic culture spread at a slower pace as defences were better. The Slavic influence increasing the pagan values. Tombstones and Stecci (head stones) are a testament to early Slavic heritage. It is only in the 9-10th century that Bosnia became open to Christian conversion by Slavic missionaries Cyril and Methodius.

The Glagolithic and Cyrillic (current) alphabets were introduced around the 9th century. The medieval period from 1180 to 1463 placed the Southern Slavs in a difficult position wedged between two great cultural and religious entities of Eastern and Western Christianity. Both the Byzantine and Rome's influence was felt in the structures of this crossroads region. The geographical position of the Southern Slavs became a key factor in the 11th century split between the Orthodox and Catholic churches. The great schism of 1040s had a profound influence in Bosnia and the Balkans region. Both Churches asserted their influence and left an indelible mark on the regions cultural history.

There developed in Bosnia a large degree of cultural resistance which resulted in a "creative mould" of Christianity. The Bosnian church was unique in the region with fierce independence from its more powerful influences. Bosnia thus maintained a high degree of secularism in its values and life. The followers of this unique church of Bosnia were called the Bogomil. Pope Benedict I in Rome attempted to use Bogomil duality as a justification for an invasion and cleansing of what was considered by the Vatican as heretics.

Medieval Bosnia was ruled by three powerful aristocrats – Ben Kulin for 24 years – 1180-1204 AD, who had delivered a golden era for Bosnia. However the Archbishop of Hungary in Split interfered in Bosnia which led to Ben Kulin's

A Stećci, a unique medieval Bosnian gravestone.

death. The Papacy actively encouraged the Hungarian church to eliminate paganism from the Bogomil church as heresy. By 1238 Hungary invaded Bosnia and failed in their attempt to establish a Dominican order. The next aristocratic period was headed by Ben Stephen – Kotromanic and which enjoyed rule for 30 years from 1322. Ben Stephen expanded his hegemony to the Dalmatian coast and the Southern Hum province thus uniting Bosnia and Herezegovinia as one political entity before he died in 1353 AD. He allowed the Vatican to establish a Fransiscan order in Bosnia and Herezegovinia, in Srebrena, thus during this time Bosnia became a Catholic state even though there were some pagan and heretic practices.

Ban Stephen was succeeded by King Stephen Tvrtko, at the young age of 15. He had a very difficult reign for the first 14 years, when he enlisted help from the Hungarian king. By 1367 Tyrtko asserted his leadership and made Bosnia the most poweful state in the West Balkans. After the death of King Tvrtko, Bosnia entered into a long period of decline and weak rule. During this decline, a new power stepped in, the Turks, who gradually took control in 1404AD. King Ostaja was driven out and replaced by King Tvrtko the Second. With the help of Hungary, Ostoja regained some control of Bosnian land. However by 1414, with increasing political and military change, regained some land, but was soon defeated by King Tvrtko 2nd, who regained the throne with help from the Ottomans. During these turbulent times in the 15th century Bosnia was influenced by two powerful forces, the Hungarians and emerging Turks.

By 1443 the Ottoman Turks intensified their attacks, this led the now weak King Stephen Tomas to appeal for help from the Papacy. It led to persecution of the Bogomil church, a very unique and self-reliant church in medieval history waned[6]. By 1528 the Bosnian kingom fell to the Turks after several failed attempts to resist by King Tomasevic (Stephen Tomas' successor).

The Sultan of Turkey assumed control of Bosnia from about 1528AD, and hence for a prolonged period Turkish influence and hegemony pervaded all aspects of life in Bosnian culture, religion and political life. The basic legal system of the Otomans did not fully abide by Islamic holy law, there was some religious tolerance and entry to the Ottoman army and work force was allowed for Christians in Bosnia. To become a "spahi" cavalry soldier paid directly by the Ottoman administration was a privilege, there were granted land and were not forced to renounce Christian beliefs in Bosnia.

Turkish "Janassaries" were the bulk of the Ottoman army, over 200,000 boys from the Balkans were recruited by the 16th century. Most of these Christian boys were freely given by their parents to the Turks to obtain land-holdings in Bosnia. Many thousands later on converted to Islam to receive privileges. The Islamisation of Bosnia was a process that lasted long and was resisted by the Slavic influence, so much so that the late Slobodan Milosvic said in 1992 that revenge was needed, collaborated by General Mladic, to redress the Ottoman intrusions of the 16-17th century. Thus deep seated enmity of the Serbs for cruelty towards the Muslims in 1991-5 have their historical origins in over 400 years of mistrust.

The wooden bridge on BentBaša in winter, Sarajevo.

The Muslim influence was major in Sarajevo and some other central areas but not in Herzegovina, which remained largely Christian, and Serb areas were Orthodox, although by late 16th century in Bosnia the demographic balance between Muslims and Christians was around 50-50. The Srebrenica community was until 1624AD mainly Ragusan and Catholic Germans. There will be a more in-depth analysis on Srebrenica in later chapters of the book.

There was a "mystical" convergence of both faiths in early Bosnia. Even to-day in Sarajevo, Christians and Muslims share the same superstitions in the power of the Amulets and many Muslims are blessed by Franciscan monks. Many holy days and religious festivals are celebrated by both. The Serbs in

10

Bosnia and in neighbouring Serbia have a very rich and interesting heritage, traced to about 1036AD when the Serbian kingdom began to emerge in present day Monternegro. Stefan Vojislav, the chief there, renounced his allegiance to the Holy Roman Emperor in Constantinople and pronounced himself for the Vatican and began to consolidate the neighboring Serb tribes under his conrol[7].

The Serbs were Slavs who migrated to the Balkans in the 4th century from the Bulgarian and Croat lands, settling in the region where the fortress of Ras was later built. Raska was another name for the Serbs, known as the Rascians. Today Raska is better known by the Turkish name of Sandzak, it conjures up Serb nationalism even to-day. The major difference between the Serb-Croats and Bosniaks (Muslims of Bosnia) are prescient in their long and difficult co-existence, which is cultural and religious. This is marked today in Bosnia, Croatia and Serbia, as they vie for association with the EU.

The arrival of the Turks in the Balkans had greater ructions than even the arrival of the Slavs in the 7th century, who preceded the Turks by about seven more turbulent centuries. As the Turks advanced the Serbs fled north towards Hungary and the Adriatic. The legacy of the later Austro-Hungarian-Turkish wars and the military frontier in the Balkans led to areas of Serb, Croat or Muslim mixed communities. This was to last till the 1991-95 Balkans Wars, where first the Croats were expelled by the Serbs and then in turn of the Serbs in Krajina by the Croats. These developments will be discussed in detail in later chapters. The Serbs suffered a cruel defeat in 1610 in the famous battle of Kosovo by the Turks. Since this defeat the Serbs have developed a mind set of revenge and strategy against the Muslims in the West Balkans both of Bosnia and Kosovo. This deep historical and religious animosity was unleashed in 1995 in Srebrenica.

The annexation of Bosnia and Herzegovina in 1908 by the Hapsburgs led to great changes in the Balkans, Bosnia, Serbia and surrounding areas. The assassination of the Arch-Duke Ferdinand, heir to the throne of the Hapsburgs by a Serb Nationalist, Princip Gavrilo in 1914 precipitated the First World War.

Bosnia has been a melting pot of Balkans politics, and after the First World War in the Treaty of Versailles in 1918, the region was formed into a Federation of Serb, Croat and Slovene, soon to be called the Kingdom of Yugoslavia.

We shall see in the next chapter the ructions of Yugoslavia, its international and domestic pressures which helped the emergence of Titoism and his Partisans and the run up to the Second World War and its aftermath and the Cold War period.

References
1 The Bradt Travel Guide - Tim Clancy 2004
2 The Bradt Travel Guide - Tim Clancy 2004
3 The Bradt Travel Guide - Tim Clancy 2004
4 The Independent April 2006
5 The Bradt Travel Guide - Tim Clancy 2004
6 The Bradt Travel Guide - Tim Clancy 2004
7 Serb history, myth and destruction of Yugoslavia – Tim Judah 1992

Chapter Three

Emergence of Titoism and its impact in Bosnia and Herzegovina

Marshall Tito was a man for his time. I feel he was at the right place at the right time and he carved up his destiny, and his legacy was huge in the West Balkans and Bosnia, Serbia and Croatia.

When Tito emerged as the supreme leader of Yugoslavia in 1950s it had six Republics, Croatia, Slovenia, Bosnia, Serbia, Montenegro and Macedonia, with Kosovo and Volvodina semi-autonomous parts of Serbia. Tito soon recognised that to keep the lid on these six republics and two semi-autonomous entities he had to introduce draconian measures of central control and strict disciplines. Tito as a Communist, and his partisans were united by a common bond of socialist ideology which differed from Stalinism. Titoism recognised that in order to unite Yugoslavia he had not only to stamp his central authority but also to uproot and weed out nationalist and ethnic sentiments in the six republics. The cost of this centralism was very dear. His department for the protection of the people (Secret Police) arrested and severely punished[2] anyone who opposed his "Brotherhood and Unity" of Socialism.

Tito's – DPP Secret Service, particularly targeted the Croats with Ustasha baggage, fellow travellers of Hitler during the World War II. It was held that nearly 250,000 Croats, Muslim and Serb "dissidents" were liquidated by the Titoist cadres. Not only ethnic groups, but religious groups like the Fransiscian clergy in Herzegovina were singled out as past supporters of the Ustasha against Tito's Partisans. Many churchs and monasteries were destroyed or closed down.

The Serb Chetniks supporters of Mihallovic who did not join the Partisans felt Titos wrath. Many Serb-Chetniks who were persecuted were isolated or left the country.

The Muslim population in Bosnia too suffered harsh punishment, and Titoists executed Muslim intellectual elites after the Second World War. Courts of Islamic sacred law were suppressed – even such religious practices like teaching children in mosques were made a criminal offence. Some Moslem women were forbidden to wear the veil and many cultural Muslim societies were closed.

13

After the expulsion by Stalin of Tito from the Comintern in 1948 Tito soon moved to a more open, inclusive and 'liberal' socialism – asserting his independence from Soviet dogma[1]. This resulted in benefits to be felt in Yugoslav Communities. Religious tolerance was encouraged, new laws were passed to allow freedom of religion, but the State/ central control of religious institutions was maintained.

There were tensions and difficulties for the Moslems under Tito, as nearly one million Muslims voted to be of "undeclared" national identity. However in the early 1960s there was some accommodation with the Muslims in Bosnia – when their nationhood was established.

Tim Clancy in 'Bradt Guide' to Bosnia says in the mid Sixties, Yugoslavia began to change its policies, where some feel the golden days of Titoism emerged when all had a job, free education, there was no homelessness, one was able to travel around the world, and some freedom was allowed even "sleeping in public parks". This was a period of rapid national renaissance. Massive infrastructural projects were evident even in Bosnia. The national roads, schools, libraries were built. The university system was extended from Sarajevo to Banja-Luka, Tuzla, Mostar, Zenice and other major cities in Bosnia.

A sense of pride and 'self-management' was given by Tito to the ethnic communities. This decentralising process, whilst very encouraging led to some damage in 1970s to the Yugoslav economy, which felt outside competition and trade pressures a heavy burden in addition to de-centralised planning formats.

Both the US and Soviet Union aided Titos Yugoslavia and in the Cold War he benefited by juggling the attention and support of both power blocs.

Tito – practised his politico-economic neutrality – which became a unique form of socialism – but not a truly democratic structure as his party and leadership was paramount even though some deregulation and devolved power was evident in the six republics. In Bosnia people had jobs, had a relatively comfortable lifestyle and freedom to work, travel and study abroad. In Croatia and Serbia nationalist sentiment in the 1970s started emerging. Some Croat and Serb leaders had visions of carving up Bosnia and integrating parts into Croatia and Serbia.

Serbian nationalism was developing faster. There was resentment by Serb nationalists to Tito's largess to the Kosovarian majority who were given an autonomous region under Yugoslavia in the late 1960s. Serbian nationalists were "obsessed" with the wish to annex Kosovo and other parts of the region into a dream of a Greater Serbia, Dobrice Cosic a Serb nationalist-communist held Serb people were harbouring the vision of a dream of unification of the scattered Serbs into a powerful single State, extending into Bosnia, Croatia and even Kosovo. Cosic was soon expelled from the Yugoslav Central Committee (Tito's). Cosic also opposed the giving of national status to the Bosnian Muslims. Even in the 1960s when Tito was holding the ethnic balance together there was anti-Islamic sentiment which was fuelled by Serbian Nationalism.

After the death of Tito, whose funeral in 1980 in Belgrade was attended by more Western and Asian and African Heads of State than for most European leaders. His place in history both in the Balkans and in the world especially in the non-aligned world in the East is assured.

Tito is still remembered in my home country of Sri Lanka, where he visited and enjoyed a great deal of good will especially amongst democratic leaders in India, Indonesia and West Africa. His place in the United Nations and his work in strengthening of the General Assembly is well known. It is an irony in history for a man of such immense stature in the UN and NAM and that by one who contributed to UN peace-keeping and humanitarian relief: a cruel coincidence later in the 1990s – only ten-twelve years after his death, the UN failed to stem the disintegration of Tito's Yugoslavia with the collapse of Communism in 1988.

Why the UN failed to prevent the Balkans wars from 1991-5 is the subject of the following chapters. It was more the reluctance of the UNSC five permanent powers and the collective apathy till 1995 of the US/EU/Western Alliance which led to much strife, death and refugees in Bosnia, Croatia and even in Kosova/Serbia.

By 1987, seven years after Tito's death poor economic times befell Yugoslavia. Inflation rose to 120% and by the next year had doubled (shades of the Weimar-Republic in Germany in the 1930s). Strikes and industrial unrest and rampant nationalism destabilised the weak economy without Tito's strong leadership. In 1989 persistent strikes in Montenegro and Volvodina in north, set the stage[3] for a new and more dangerous Serbian Communist leader the late Slobodan Milosevic.

In 1989 Milosevic cleverly manipulated the party apparathicks. The Serbian Assembly passed a constitutional amendment that abolished the autonomy of Kosovo and Volvodina. This led to massive opposition

War destroyed home, Sarajevo 1993-95 (Ljbujanska).

in Kosovo, this protest was dealt with by the Serbian security forces led by Milosevic.

Tito's legacy was flawed according to Nora Beloff - a well known Observer journalist for 27 years. According to Nora Beloff, Tito's role in the making of 'present day' Yougoslavia was grossly misunderstood in the West.[4] Nora Beloff is of the view that Tito and his partisans were determined to emerge as the victors (Communists) after the Second World War. She is of the view that Tito and the Chetnik leader Milhaillovic had a built in antipathy based on power. She goes on to state that Tito systematically destroyed all potential opposition, even to the point of weakening the war effort against the Germans. She says Churchill and Roosevelt were misguided and misinformed of Tito's intentions.

Nora Beloff seems to write more in sorrow than in anger, more in hope than despair. She is not hostile to Yugoslav emergence after World War Two. She is of the view that in the West, one looked at Tito and his achievement with rose-coloured glasses.

I believe Tito's place in Yugoslav and world history is secured inspite of Beloff's belated "histrionics". Tito was held in high esteem in Asia, Africa and also Cuba, where poverty allieviation and empowerment were more important than pure rhetorical Western concepts of democracy and power. Neither do I agree with Nora Beloff that after forty years of Titoism, the cultural and ethnic cleavages have been deepened by Tito.

I am of the view, to be discussed further in the latter chapters of this book, that Tito's legacy was more unifying than destructive, and till early 1980s he kept the centrifugal forces of Bosnia/Serb/Croat rivalries from spilling over into an earlier bloodbath than the now familiar three Balkan wars of 1991-5.

Let me now focus on the next chapter, on the collapse of the Berlin Wall and the end of the Soviet Union, its consequences for the EU and the Balkans in particular where with Tito's death – nationalism was emergent.

War ruins, Sarajevo 1992-95 (Ljbujanska).

After the demise of Tito and the slow disintegration of former Yugoslavia there was a large degree of economic and technological self management and deregulation in the Six Republics especially Serbia, Croatia and Bosnia and Herzegovina.

The centrally controlled party apparatus of Tito was collapsing by 1985-6, new economic determinism and private investment were changing management styles and control in the Republics. This process led to major effects on the political and institutional structures, it led to ethnic determinism and weaker central control. This led to Serbia and Croatia rather than Bosnia being run by Technocrats and Oligarchic tendencies than Party apparatus.

Both Miloselvic and Tudjman and to a lesser degree Alija Izetbegovic and Haris Sladjzic were able to exert control due to technical specialisms instead of sheer Titoist party affinity. These new tendencies exacerbated the disintegration process of Former Yugoslavia and led to rabid nationalism and regional specificity away from the centrally controlled Republics.[5]

By 1990 most of the Republics were ready to assert their independence, which hastened the commencement of the three Balkans wars of 1991-5.

References

1 'The future of Communism in Eastern Europe' John. W. Young
2 Bradt Guide on Bosnia and Herzegovina – Tim Clancy
3 Bradt Guide on Bosnia – Tim Clancy 2004.
4 'Titos Yugoslavia' 1939-1984 Nora Beloff
5 'Global Governance in 21st Century' – Mike Duffield 2005

Chapter Four

Collapse of the Soviet Union and Communism and Rabid Nationalism in the West Balkans

The collapse of the Soviet Union in 1988 and the fall of the Berlin Wall heralded a new, exciting and yet dangerous period in international relations in the world and in particular in the Balkans.

The Warsaw pact and the Communist grip on its client states weakened, from Poland to Latvia to former Yugoslavia and Hungary, these areas felt seismic changes in the political architecture of Eastern and Central European and Baltic States.

President Gorbachev's twin-tract reforms of Glasnost[1] and Perestroika[2] led to confusion and rapid upheavals throughout the Soviet Union and beyond. President Yeltsin soon acted to salvage the power of the Russian Federation after Gorbachev and a chain of political and economic convulsions followed in Eastern and Central Europe including in former Yugoslavia.

Yugoslavia which had under Tito fiercely resisted and fashioned a new socialism at first did not directly feel the collapse of the USSR. However with the global balance of power shifting to an unipolar western alliance led by the United States, resulting in opportunities and threats for former Yugoslavia, and its new nationalist leaders. Strong and clever leaders like Milosevic of Serbia and Franco Tudjman of Croatia, asserted their independence and started a process of the carving up of parts of Bosnia and Herzegovina with military and economic aggrandisement in sympathy with some EU countries like Germany openly supporting Croatia and the French, Greeks and to a lesser extent Britain in empathy with Serb-Nationalism, these intentions were more due to loyalties arising out of World War II and not due to political exploitation.

The direct result of the break-up of the once centrally controlled Yugoslavian federation of Tito, was its inability to withstand the fierce national and regional ambitions of Croatia, Serbia, Slovena and to a lesser extent Bosnia and Macedonia. The FYSR was now dead, and there arose long and fierce and damaging three Balkans wars from 1991-1995.

Slovenia asserted independence with the blessing of Austria and Italy her new EU Neighbours, after a short 'war', the Serb leadership now under Slobadan Milosevic inherited most of the fire power and valuable military assets of the J.N.A. (National Yugoslavia Army) agreed to Slovenia's independence and soon the U.N. and E.U. recognised the new small state as the first of six ex-Yugoslav Republics.

In the case of Croatia, Serbia and Bosnia there were ancient and deep rooted cultural and politico-economic reasons for the disintegration of trust and desire to work or "live" together unlike under Tito.

Ironically Tito's model of Socialism not as virulent in its economic/political control as the Comintern of Stalin, sowed the seeds of its own destruction. Under Tito, each of the six constituent republics were devolved economic and decentralised political activity, which encouraged not only greater nationalism but also for a new generation of passionate and fiercely regional leaders like Milosevic in Serbia, Tudjman of Croatia and Alija Izetbegovic in Bosnia and Herzegovina who found the 1989-90 period an opportunity to break up the centrally controlled federation of former Yugoslavia.

1991-1995 saw the emergence of a cruel, calluous and most inhuman nationalist cultural and ethnic hatred being reaped by the new leadership in that region, freed of the influence of Soviets and Tito and the aftermath of World War II. There arose a period of ethnic, religious and national fervour which devoured the West Balkans. Old neighbours and friends became enemies and it led to a dark and damaging four years of hardship and instability for the peoples of the once unified six republics.

The ancient cultural, religious and ethnic differences of the Slav-Serbs Turkish-Bosnian and "Germanic" Croats, who were joined in a common bond by Tito and other factors of the 1960s and the 1980s – surfaced to the fore with a vengence, the leaders of these three new countries exploited and manipulated the cultural and ethnic differences and sensitivities that had been bottled up for hundreds of years, erupted with a vengence. Events like Vukavor, Krajina, Srebrenica, Zepa, and even Sarajevo siege were inhuman and irrational behaviours of a once "unified and cohesive Yugoslavia".

To realise the dream of a Greater/ Pure Serbia with Slavic history and culture; leaders like Milosevic and General Mladic have said the Bosnian Muslims were "dogs" left over from the Ottoman Turkish invasion in the 15th century. Deep divisions, culture, history, religion and economic fears were used in the early 1990s to justify the three cruel Balkan wars which led to over one million deaths, over three million refugees and internal displaced persons in an area and state once "unified" by Tito.

Srebrenica/Potocari Memorial and
Great Marble Wall of all war victims names .
(LA Digital Photos)

It is not ironic or by sheer coincidence that Srebrenica happened in 1995. But it was "culturally" inevitable. The propensity for cruelty and brutality remains unexplained, but now calling themselves Independent and assertive to the extent of Mladic Milosevic, Karadzic Tudjman and some Muslim Bosniacs were "demonising" the old historical divisions and prejudices of the Slavs, Ottomans, Hapsburgs, Germans and once Communists.

It is a small wonder that the three Balkans wars led to ferocious and inhuman and cruel "massacres" like in Vukavor and Srebrenica where the population mix and demographic balance ethnically and religious divisions were very fine.

From the sixth century Slav "dominance" and then Ottoman hegemony and latter day mistrust led to a culture of revenge and retribution. It is alledged to justify and to let the Bosnian Serbs and Bosnian-Muslims tragically make it happen, compounded worse by the inability of the UN and EU to act earlier.

In summary I am of the view in 1994, if the US and EU acted decisively with NATO that the Srebrenica tragedy could have been avoided or at least mitigated and the wars in the West Balkans could have been stopped before the Dayton Accords in December 1995, when the wanton damage pushed the International Community to act, to prevent it spilling over to the East Balkans and beyond.

References
1 Glasnost – policy of openness and accountability
2 Perestroika – policy of re-structuring of the economy and political system (Gorbachev reforms)

Chapter Five

UN Protection force (UNPROFOR) its early probelms and later successes in Bosnia and Herzegovina

The UNPROPOR was established by the UNSC in 1991, first as an observer mission on the recommendation of Cyrus Vance, when the fighting broke out in East Croatia, between the Serb forces and the Croats.

UNPROFOR was preceded by an (UNMCOY) UN observer/ monitoring force in 1991, after Cyrus Vance negotiated a fragile cease fire between President Milosevic and Tudjman and the Serb-Bosnians after the fall of Vukovor, the first great advance and capture by the Serb-Bosnian forces of the Croat area after much damage[1].

It was apparent to the UNSC that a mere monitoring force was not adequate to observe, monitor or "hold the line" in East Slavonia as the Serbs had overwhelming fire power having acquired the vastly superior military assets of the J.N.A. (Yugoslavian national army) after the disintegration of the federation.

With the recognition of Croatia as a sovereign independent state in 1990-1 by the Germans and then the EU and UN, pressure was mounting diplomatically to help Tudjman – the new President there who was faced by the full exposure to the superior forces of Serbia. The UNSC, rightly established UNPROFOR, to help diffuse the now escalating and increasing threat from Serbia to the peace and security in the West Balkans.

Whilst the P5 (Permanent 5) of the UNSC made the right decision, it failed in its judgment on the "limited" mandate for the force, and also its equally limited resources: UNPROFOR went in 1991 to former Yugoslavia with a weak mandate, and even weaker command and control structure under-funded and under-manned. It was a protection force.

The first UNPROFOR/ UNMLOY[2] was about 8500 personnel, widely dispersed and ill-equipped and hastily fitted out to tackle a dangerous area in the heart of Europe. This was compounded by the lack of support for the force from neither the EU or NATO who should have been more ideally placed to tackle the mounting military/ political problems of FYSR.

After the escalation of the conflict in Former Yugoslavia, UNPROFOR was up-rated by the UNSC in 1992 to a force of nearly 17000 personnel drawn up from 27 countries including nine countries which sent observers. Why with such support and numbers did UNPROFOR fail in the early years?

This is not due to its ground troops or local command, but due inherently to the weak mandate and lack of support. These were long debates and disagreement in the UNSC on the early control and logistical support for the force. The inability of the force command and control to understand the UNSC and also lack of direct support/ co-ordination from the EU contact group of countries and the early fears of the Russian federation on intervention by UN in their once sphere of influence, made the effectiveness of the force marginal in its early days. Confusion resulted, was it an observer force or peace-keeping or peace enforcement? These areas were not clearly defined by the UNSC and the Secretary-General.

Block of flats, near Holiday Inn Hotel, war damaged, 1992-93.

By 1992 when the conflict in West Balkans spread to Bosnia and Herzegovina, UNPROFOR had a very challenging task both humanitarian and peace-keeping bordering on peace enforcement. The Secretary-General

Boutros-Boutros Ghali had long and somewhat difficult discussions with the Security Council. Due to political and ideological and strategic factors in the UN, UNPROFOR lacked a clear sense of purpose and direction in former Yugoslavia. It became also the victim of Big Power antipathy and discord, between UN foreign policy and E.U. indecision which affected the morale and ethos of the ground operation entrusted to UNPROFOR.

Whilst there were effective and capable leaders like Lieutenant General Lewis MacKenzie; Philippe Morillion; Lieutenant General Nambiar and diplomats like Cyrus Vance, Cedric Thornberry and Kofi-Annan then deputy Secretary General for UN peace-keeping; The UN inherently suffered from lack of direction and clear objectives in the West Balkans conflicts which they felt was essentially an European matter.

The US early fatigue with the Gulf invasion, abortive action in Somalia and weak action in Haiti and its domestic politics, where the Bush administration was still suffering from the "Vietnam albatross" did not help a clear and decisive approach in former Yugoslavia. Some were of the belief that the U.S. did not wish to engage in essentially a "European" problem neither did they feel the UN should be given adequate resources to tackle a post-cold war problem, internal ructions in former Yugoslavia carved up by ambitious Nationalists Politicians in Serbia, Croatia, and Bosnia and Herzegovina.

Boutros-Boutros Ghali was over-burdened and not a popular Secretary General particularly with his own personnel and more importantly with the U.S. administration. The Secretary General said in 1991, the UN was faced with running seventeen different operations for peace missions with 70,000 personnel in the field. The Secretary-General said "we needed $3 billion as states collapsed, war crimes proliferated and genocide raged.[3]

According to Lieutenant General MacKenzie of UNPROFOR there was early confusion about the location of the HQ of UNPROFOR. The diplomats in New York and the field commanders could not agree even though the latter seem to know what they were doing or seeking to do whilst the soldiers were supposed to listen to the diplomats. The question of Zagreb to be the base for the 14,000 UNPROFOR personnel was not a popular or a logistically correct one. It was felt Belgrade or Sarajevo would be a better logistical option.

By 1992, the Vance plan had collapsed and the second Balkans war was rapidly engulfing that of Bosnia and Herzegovina after she declared

Plaque of the burning of the National Library, 28/8/92.

independence. President Izetbegovic who had been placed in a "lose-lose" situation[4] held a referendum to consult the people on independence. The Muslims and Croats of Bosnia and Herzegovina chose independence, while the Serb-Bosnians boycotted it. The Serb-Bosnians – Radovan Karadzic and General Mladic wanted to establish their own Bosnian-Serb semi state (entity) within Bosnia-Herzegovina, with some link to Serbia. Tensions were now very high between the Bosnian Muslims and Serb-Bosnians.

Into this political and military cauldron UNPROFOR tip-toed without prior direction and inadequate resources and personnel. By 1992-4 UNPROFOR was faced with a huge dilemma – how to contain or even carry out its much changed mandate which had been revised 64 times by the UNSC The Serb-Bosnians with support from Serbia were advancing both on Bosnia-Herzegovina and Croat outposts. UNPROFOR was no longer an observer force or peace keeping force as there was no 'Truce or Peace' to keep. It had to support the increasingly diverse role of humanitarian assistance to both UNHCR and ICRC, when millions of refugees and IDP's were moving from their homes to escape the wrath of the Serbs and even Croats in their intensified battles for supremacy.

By late 1994 UNPROFOR was so stretched that there was a debate in the UNSC whether it be withdrawn from the West Balkans. However due to enlarged duties of the 1993 Safe Areas, UNPROFOR had to be diverted to more humanitarian work than peace enforcement or peace keeping. UNPROFOR suffered not only inadequate resources but also from a confused and diverse mandate. Here the UNSC should be blamed for this confusion and indecision.

There were several "Peace Initiatives" first by Cyrus Vance, then Vance-Owen and Stoltenberg and Owen, which were joint approaches on behalf of the UN and the E.U. The latter now took an increasingly active role through the contact group of five countries of Germany, France, U.K., U.S. and Russia who were faced by the escalation of the Balkans war to its third and more virulent phase.

Lieutenant General MacKenzie in his book "Road to Sarajevo" says there were two agendas in Bosnia and Herzegovina. The Bosnian Serbs led by Radovan Karadzic and aided by Serbia, wanted their own mini-state with a green line, manned by the UN separating them from the rest of the Bosnian Muslims, whereas President Izetbegovic of the Muslims wanted international military intervention. In fact by 1993-4 the Serb-Bosnians had annexed nearly 70% of the land of Bosnia and Herzegovina by their military action both against Bosnian Muslims and Bosnian Croats in the West.

The Serb-Bosnians in their HQ in Pale had established their ethnic Republika Sprksa which was to join up with a corridor in Srebrenica area to a greater Serbia. This territorial delineation alarmed both the Contact group, UN and even Milosevic himself who felt the Muslims and Croat ethnic communities were being boxed in by ethnic and political cleansing from Pale.

It is most interesting how, when the UN economic sanctions were beginning to bite, Milosevic used his influence to bargain with the West to 'isolate' his Serb-Bosnian ally Karadizic's plans for expansion in Bosnia.

The UN and E.U. with the help of NATO used several methods to bear down upon both Milosevic and the Republika Sprksa of Pale. No fly zones, heavy weapon exclusion zones and safe havens were being increasingly used to mitigate the Serb advances not only into the now fully exposed Muslim-Croat Federation in Bosnia, all these measures were well intended but were inadequately controlled. This direction from the UNSC to UNPROFOR was found wanting, more so with the mandate problems there, what was needed was peace enforcement with a credible threat of force against the Serb-Bosnians and Milosevic, with NATO air support.

In addition to internal wrangling and lack of direction, UNPROFOR suffered from not adequate liason with NATO, who had the fire-power and adequate ability to provide a clear threat to safeguard the Safe Areas.

I shall in the next chapter, elucidate the causes and effects of the failed UN Safe Areas. In the meantime, let us focus on some of the successes and pluses of UNPROFOR in the 1993-5 period before the Dayton Peace Accords.

UNPROFOR had some success as an humanitarian force, providing UNHCR and ICRC personnel with cover and assistance in dealing with movement of food-stuffs, medical supplies, water and other essentials especially in the prolonged Sarajevo siege and also protection of convoys of large amount of material, refugees and IDP's who were under the care of UNHCR. Here the UN performed very well and as always the case, was an example for solace and comfort to many thousands of refugees in the west Balkans, in particular Bosnia.

UNPROFOR under Lewis McKenzie, Michael Rose and others – were able to hold and keep open Sarajevo International airport which was an area constantly bombarded by Serb-Bosnian heavy artillery.

We need to look in the next chapter on the dynamics and the logic of the UN safe areas which UNPROFOR had to supervise, here they were several weakness not only in its mandate limitations but also the lack of an adequately resourced force, which still lacked a credible threat to the Serb-Bosnians who by 1993-4 were on the ascendancy in Bosnia Herzegovina, engaged in considerable ethnic, political and administrative cleansing.

To conclude this chapter, on hind-sight UNPROFOR was hastily convened, badly mandated at least in its early life, it was grossly under-resourced both with inadequate ground troops and lacking in armour or air support cover, which NATO could have provided.

In addition Secretary General Bontros Ghali had problems both with the UNSC and the U.S. administration and also his own personnel in New York and at the sharp end force commanders.

It suffered also from lack of co-operation from the E.U. and also due to previous set-backs of the P5 members of the UNSC, in other conflict zones like Somaili, Haiti and Rwanda and Burundi. Mat Berdal[5] says the UNSC's handling of the war in Bosnia and Herzegovina remains one of the most controversial of all its efforts to deal with violent conflicts since the end of the cold war. UNPROFOR's great failure was the inability to protect the safe area of Srebrenica, which we shall fully focus in later chapters.

It is relevant to draw the readers attention to how the five permanent members of the UNSC were blamed for the failure of UNPROFOR in its primary objective of peace in West Balkans.

The US administration wanted direct action backed by air power, with NATO involvement but was hindered by the U.S. Congress who were cagey of direct intervention even by the UN after their set backs in Somalia and Haiti.

New building of British Council, Ljbujanska,
Sarajevo, where I did a lot of my research.

In the case of Britain and France, they had somewhat contradictory foreign policy on Bosnia. The U.K. government under Prime Minister John Major was split too and also engrossed in difficult Maastricht treaty negotiations. Britain favoured safe areas and no fly zones, but was not supportive of NATO close air support for UNPROFOR. France on the other hand had under President Mitterand an inconsistent foreign policy of first favouring Serbia a close ally during World War II, and later supporting a massive humanitarian intervention to alleviate the Sarajevo siege, and to open Sarajevo airport. Under President Chirac, France fully embraced a very tough stand against the Serb excesses and supported the idea of a 'rapid reaction force' with NATO air support, moreover the Safe Havens concepts was mainly French in conceptual terms.

In the case of Russia and China, both these P5 powers took a pragmatic and less doctrinaire stand on Bosnia. The former, under President Yeltsin was keen to obtain western credits for his liberalised economy and did not feel happy to jeopardise it by meddling in former Yugoslavia, a sphere of influence in which even the mighty Soviet Union were unable to have hegemony due to Tito.

The P5 were split and was unable tragically to give a clear direction in the West Balkans the same could be said of the EU where the Germans in particular favoured Croatia, and the French and Greeks to a lesser extent supporting Serbia; whilst Britain "sat on the fence" to the detriment of the Bosnian Muslims who did not have much patronage in the UNSC. All these factors had a telling impact on UNPROFOR's general failure.

References

1 UN Peace-keeping in trouble, Lessons learned in former Yugoslavia, Edited – Wolfgang, Brerman and Martin Vadset 1998.
2 UNMLOY United Nations Military Liason Officers Yugoslavia.
3 Boutros Ghali Book 'Unvanquished' – Memoirs
4 Lieutenant General Lewis MacKenzie "Road to Sarajevo"
5 Mat Berdal Eds. "Peace-keeping, chapter 20, p.p. 45

Chapter Six

UN Safe havens "Areas" in Bosnia Herzegovina; and the Vance-Owen Peace Plan

Before we discuss the dynamics and the whole failure of UN 'Safe Areas' let us briefly look at the VOPP[1] and SOP[2] for Bosnia-Herzegovina.

The VOPP, well crafted by Cyrus Vance and David Owen on behalf of the UN and E.U. was a solution to restore peace in Bosnia but it lacked the tacit agreement of the major players like President Izetbegovic and his Prime Minister Haris Silajdzic and Radovan Karadzic who held differing positions and passions on the work Vance and Owen, who did to bring it to the negotiating table. In addition the E.U. Contact group and UNSC did not forcefully back the logic of VOPP.

The Serb-Bosnians were entrenched in the Republika Sprksa with an unequal territorial advantage. The Pale administration did not favour the cantonisation plan of Vance-Owen, even though the Muslim leadership may have benefited by the VOPP – where they could have acquired a greater amount of land and territory than what the federation eventually got from the Dayton Accords.

The SOP proposals too suffered from lack of clarity and the Serb-Bosnian mistrust. It is very tragic that both VOPP and SOP were sacrificed more due to lack of will by the UN/EU posturing, which again led to the escalation of the war in Bosnia and the fall of Srebrenica, Zepa and also the prolonged siege and damage to Sarajevo.

The Safe Areas in Bosnia conceptually were weak, both in theory and practice, in two principal ways. First, they were more a deterrent as a diplomatic measure, than as a strategic war measure. Secondly, without NATO fire power, safe havens were untenable in practice as UNPROFOR neither had adequate fire-power or air support to defend the six areas.

In addition the Serb-Bosnians over-whelming advantage of artillery pieces and heavy guns made these safe areas "sitting ducks", with weak Muslim artillery but perhaps enough infantry poorly armed and buttressed by a weak and ineffective Dutch Peace Keepers of UNPROFOR as was the case in Zepa and latter in Srebrenica in 1993-5 period to the virulent Serb-Bosnian on-slaughts.

The safe areas implementation ran into major difficulties as initially, only few countries offered to make additional troops available to meet even the "light minimum option" of 7600 that had been designated to UNPROFOR by the Security Council.[3] More than just inadequate battalion availablility (the Dutch battalion arrived in 1994) there were disagreements between the Security Council members about appropriate policy towards Bosnia and Herzegovina, arising from these political and diplomatic misgivings arose serious military and political failures by the UN in dealing with the Serb-Bosnians and even the Muslims who had differing perceptions of the concept and validity of UN Safe areas.

The flaw with Resolution 836 (4/6/1993) was that it was a short-term "sticking plaster" measure, to stave off a serious humanitarian situation, and than the longer term diplomatic or strategic objective of peace was not fully addressed, or were diluted between the Council and the E.U and force commanders on the ground who were increasingly burdened by lack of resources and strategic focus, in policing adequately the six "safe areas".

The U.S. in 1993 – especially presidential candidate Bill Clinton promised tough military action against the Serb-Bosnian aggression, but after he became President was hampered by Congress indecision and inability to put U.S. words into cohesive action, especially after U.S. humiliating set backs in Somalia and Haiti. Lord David Hannay former U.K. ambassador to UNSC says a "more robust and less vulnerable policy" was not adopted in Bosnia before summer 1995.[4] This luke-warm policy was due to tensions between those member states of UN with troops on the ground and those like the U.S. without any troops, when they were needed to defend the 'safe areas'.

Whilst the U.S. fiddled in internal debate and indecision towards Bosnia's safe areas due to Republican/Democratic arguments in the U.S. Congress; Russia, under President Boris Yeltsin, did not show the expected support to the Serb-Bosnians. Whilst there was sentiment toward 'Slavic brotherhood' by and large Russia wanted to assert her new position after the collapse of the Soviet Union and much of the Russian Federation foreign policy was one of constructive engagement towards the West in order to obtain massive economic and trading concessions both from the E.U. and the U.S. Russia in the UNSC played a very tactical role on Bosnia and safe areas, much like

Britain and France, who again showed differing strategic interests in delivering resolution 836 and safe areas. China the other P5 major power showed very little real interest in the Bosnian crisis, and felt it was a European problem where European solutions should be sought rather than for a global UN solution.

Hence the whole 'safe areas' concept whilst conceived in honour, lacked credibility and bite from its inception, in fact it increased the Serb and Serb-Bosnian resolve to attack and negate the safe havens as both unreasonable, and heavily biased against their ethnic populations particularly in Srebrenica and Sarajevo.

What of the Muslim-Bosnians and Croat Bosnians – view of the efficacy of the UN safe areas? Firstly the Croat Bosnians were not affected or involved directly with UN safe areas, other than pure logistical factors. There were no safe havens, in Croat areas even though in Herzegovina and Morstar, these may have been justified.

In the case of the Muslim Bosnian population, they suffered enormous reprisals and harm from the full onslaught by the Serb forces from 1992

*Exterior of war damaged Town Hall
and National Library, BentBaša, Sarajevo 26/8/1992*

onwards as soon as Bosnia declared independence. Whilst President Izetbegovic received a mandate in the referendum for a sovereign state, with recognition by the UN and E.U. in 1992, they were ill-equipped to face the intensity of battle by Serb-Bosnians who had both Serbia and the J.N.A. fire power behind them.

In 1992-93, the Serbs inflicted considerable damage on the Muslim population in Eastern Bosnia in particular and with a prolonged siege on Sarajevo. Food supplies were affected and ammunition and arms were hampered due to the inequity of the UN arms embargo.

It is said whilst the Muslim Bosnians had men ready to fight to defend their new state, they had primitive armour and some rifles from the first world war and even hunting rifles. They had little artillery or aircraft to defend themselves, and the military and even political leadership in early struggles were not united. President Izetbegovic was not as dynamic or strategically clever as his Serb-Bosnian counterparts, though he had younger and more assertive leaders like Prime Minister Haris Silajdzic and two very able Foreign Ministers especially Minister Scribley who had diplomatic clout with Western leaders in particular in the first Clinton administration.

What they lacked in military might, the Muslim Bosnians made up in diplomatic engagements. Very soon as the Serb onslaught affected them, they appealed for help from the UN and the E.U. The French under both Mitterand and Chirac pushed the concept of safe havens for the beleaguered Muslims both in Sarajevo, Zepa and later in Srebrenica
when it fell into the hands of General Mladic and advancing Serb forces. Nearly a million refugees and IDP's were on the move from Muslim villages both to Sarajevo and abroad. There was a humanitarian catastrophe in Muslim areas, where water, food stuffs and medical supplies were short.

The UN by 1993, and surprisingly passed several resolutions including the famous resolution 836 to declare six areas as safe havens, and vested UNPROFOR the responsibility of policing and protecting the people in East Bosnia.

There was a great humanitarian logistical case for the action of the UNSC, but did they over-react and then compound matters by not giving the UNPROFOR commanders on the ground adequate resources and lack of close air support.

The UNSC intention was good but again it was only tactical and not strategically well thought out. They made six areas into safe havens when perhaps three would have been militarily not required. Certainly Gorazde, Tuzla and Bihac should have been fortified by the Muslim forces and given the wherewithal to fight. Only Zepa, Sarajevo and of course Srebrenica, to my mind justified immediate safe area status.

SCHEMATIC MODEL OF A SAFE AREA

(UNPROFOR Concept of Implementation
SCR 824, dated 10 May 1993 – Annex of a
fax sent to the UNHQ by the Force
Commander requiring additional troops
to implement the Zones of Separation
around Safe Areas)

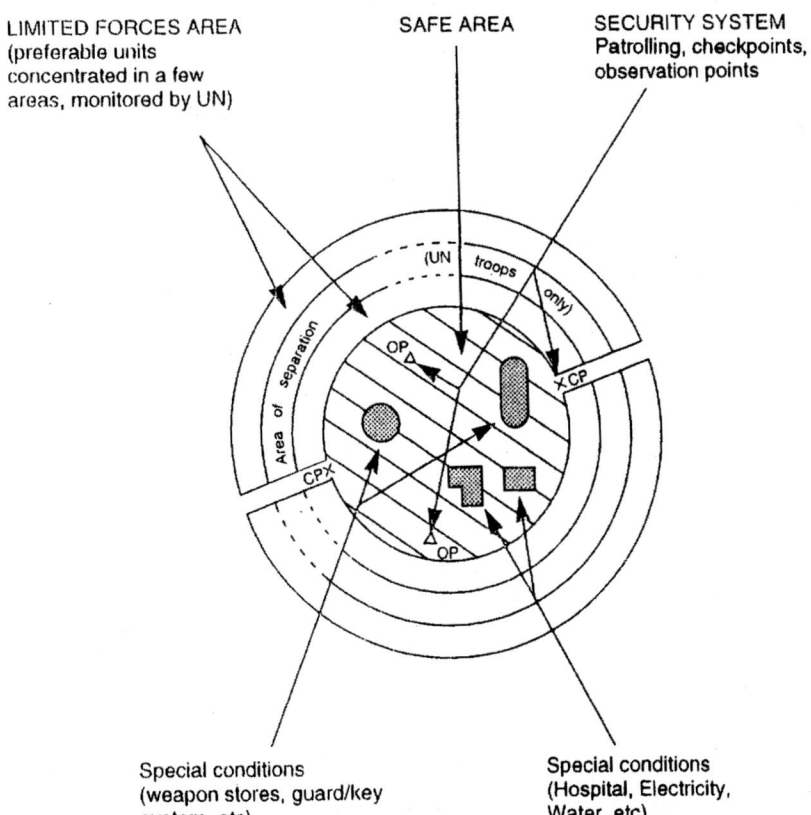

LIMITED FORCES AREA
(preferable units
concentrated in a few
areas, monitored by UN)

SAFE AREA

SECURITY SYSTEM
Patrolling, checkpoints,
observation points

Special conditions
(weapon stores, guard/key
system, etc)

Special conditions
(Hospital, Electricity,
Water, etc)

UN Safe Area (courtesy of UNPROFOR).

Again UNPROFOR was over-stretched because in reality they needed a force of over 30,000 to protect the six areas and even then would have needed air support and the enforcement of no fly zones to be underwritten by NATO.

The great UN mystery was why were these essential logistics and fire power and air power not provided. The E.U. contact group vacillated and left the 'big' decisions to the UNSC, partly due to Bloc politics, and partly due to the lack of adequate funding for UNPROFOR.

The UN forces, particularly the 'infamous' Dutch Bat in Srebrenica was so ill-equipped and riven by political interference from their masters in Holland,

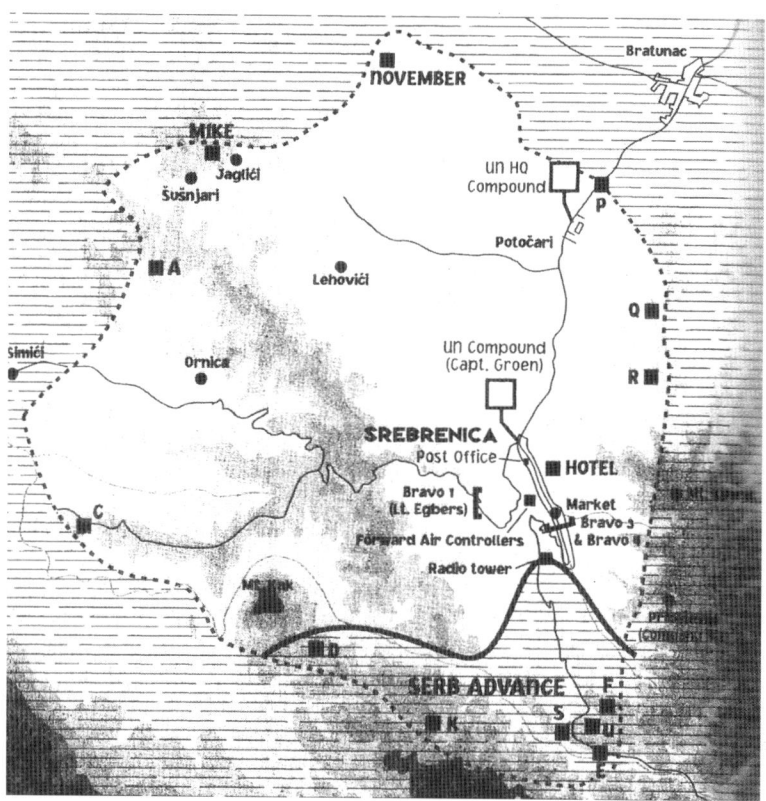

Srebrenica Safe Area 11/7/1995
Courtesy of "End Game" pp176, David Rohde.

that it was small wonder that they became hostages for peace and were at the mercy of Serb forces in both Zepa and Srebrenica.

Overall the safe areas were good in concept, but very weak in strategy and did not alleviate the suffering of the affected Muslim peoples, only the humanitarian aspect of safe areas worked thanks to some heroic work by both some advance units of UNPROFOR who provided valuable convoy and reconnaissance cover for UNHCR and the ICRC in coping with migration problems of the refugees and the IDP's.

Srebrenica Record, courtesy of British Council, Bosnia Herzegovina.

The Serbs were infuriated by the concept of six safe areas even in Gorazde and Bihac, where they felt their minorities were not protected by UNPROFOR, who were wrongly accused of preferring protection to the Muslim majority. The concept of safe areas was intended to protect and defend the whole population of those areas.

Here again UNPROFOR, perhaps unjustly is held to have only "defended" the Muslim Bosnians and as was evident in 1994 in Bihac and Gorazde when the first sign of Serb casualties were evident. Both in Bihac and Gorazde the Muslim forces were better prepared and also with the second front opened up by the now stronger and fortified Croat forces inflicting sweeping damage on Serb positions in Krajina district the case for a rapid peace process was mounted in the diplomatic front in 1995.

We shall have in chapter eight and chapter nine an in depth analysis on the fall of Srebrenica and massacre in 1995. Then evaluate how the safe area concept failed to prevent the great July tragedy of Srebrenica which shocked and jerked the international community into full alert after such a ghastly event. Let us know turn to Chapter 7, the Great Sarajevo Seige.

References
1 Vance-Owen Peace Plan
2 Stoltenberg-Owen Plan
3 Mats Bersdale – Peacekeeping in Bosnia Eds.
4 Lord David Hannay – leading article on UN Safe areas, Oxford International affairs, 1996.

Potocari Memorial and the Author, July 2006.

Chapter Seven

Sarajevo Beckons

As my book is partly dedicated to all Sarajevans past and present, I feel I need to write about that wonderful city, granted great city status in 1992, eight years after the successful winter Olympic games, which showed the organisational flair and beauty of that city to the sporting world. It is a great city steeped in history, from the medieval Byzantine to the 19-20th century and the post modern period of today.

I was able to enjoy Sarajevo the capital city of Bosnia and the Sarajevan friendship and hospitality in peace time in July 2006. But many before me have visited that city in the midst of trauma, conflict and in times of desperate straits.

Sarajevo as an international city, the capital of Bosnia and Herzegovina has been over-run, and influenced from the 15th century by the Ottoman Turks, the Austro-Hungarians, the Nazis and more recently suffered calamitous damage in 1992 – 1995 period under incessant Serb bombardment in the last Balkans war.

As most of us know Sarajevo where the Serb assassin Carlos Philippe fired a shot for "liberty" against the Austro-Hungarian Empire, which precipitated the First World War. During the uneasy peace between the Two Great World Wars, Sarajevo grew into a 'jewel' in Central Europe and then 47 years later suffered a siege of such great magnitude, that has shaken its fabric, its people and its way of life.

In 1992-5 it was under the constant and relentless attack by Serb forces – encircling the hills that surround the valley and the great river Miltjcka and 30 odd bridges of the Sarajevo district.

It was only with the help of UNPROFOR and UNHCR and ICRC and other organisations that the 600,000 citizens and many more refugees survived without water, electricity, food and medical supplies. During this period, the resolve and spirit of Sarajevans was phenomenal, children old and young survived on little, on pigeon meat and vegetable leaves, not much fruit, bread, eggs or meat or even milk.

The Sarajevans had to live in holes, basements and tunnels, and came out at night to gather what little water and sustenance with the help of the UN and other humanitarian agencies that helped them through in their darkest period. Schools, trams, hospitals, cinemas and other normal amenities stopped.

How did they survive? I was fortunate in July 2006 only 12-14 years after one of the worst sieges in Europe, to share in those memories re-told to me by young and old, what kept them alive, on their survival instinct and sense of family and community and their faith in Allah and Christ and their traditions proudly connected to centuries.

Sarejevo – helicoper shot down – at History Museum, 1994.

They told me stories, which are incredibly brave and comparable to the resistance of the little Viet-Cong/ Vietnamese against the mighty American bombardment in the 1960s-1970s in Indo-China. The Sarajevans learned that if they held together a day at a time, a week, a month and a year, would make them stronger, and they did for nearly four dark years before the Serb siege was lifted with the help of the UN forces and later NATO.

Their memories are bleak and some are angry but not depressed, they have regenerated Sarajevo since 1995, a small miracle has happened there. I was proud and privileged to see it in 2006. To me the city will remain as one of the most beautiful cities in the world, a cross between Istanbul, Rome, Moscow, and Vienna in its cultural and architectural splendour – it is the "Jerusalem of the Balkans".

The people of Sarajevo are special for me. I was their friend to some, an "Indian man" to others a British "professor", and yet to a few, a Sri Lankan Buddhist traveller not a terrorist, as they had heard of our cruel civil war in Sri Lanka, the suicide bombers, and our ahimsa doctrine in Buddhism.

As I was a researcher, learning and talking to them of the tragic events of Srebrenica, I had the good fortune of being welcome, very welcome, and I felt for them, for their pain, their anguish and more importantly for their future to be part of the European Union.

I left Sarajevo Airport with a heavy heart, yet a fulfilled heart, treasuring what I saw, the food and the warmth of the people, and not the fractured past which they have to bear. I felt I shall return by next year, with my book and share it with the city folk, to let them share in my hopes and aspirations for their future.

Aisa Telalovic, Information Manager of
British Council, Sarajevo, and me.

I have collected, both by curtesy of the British Council in Sarajevo and other sources, some valuable stories and anecdotes and many digital photos which I took and which I wish to share with my readers in the book.

Some interviews and discussions informally held late night whilst I stayed in a small hotel. Some of these comments are unattributable and given to me in confidence and in all sincerity by young people all under 25-30 years whose views and opinions I shall respect:

"Never mind where you are, only

1. important who you are with
2. we have nearly a seventh sense, have survived much and look to our future with hope"
3. "Our Education system is not empowering us"
4. "Administrative systems are bureaucratic and full of red tape.
5. "There is a degree of nepotism in the job markets
6. "New technology and research material not used in public sector. Inland Revenue Department is weak, and Government Exchequer loses much revenue due to bureaucracy.
7. Economy now in downturn after 2003-4, low growth, rising inflation, high interest rates, and very high youth unemployment.
8. The structure of Republika Sprska, the Federation of Bosnia and Croats, and multi-tiered civil service – of over 3-4 layers inhibiting growth and sense of one nation.
9. Political elites and civil structures are again remote from people, three presidents and many administrative levels delay projects/ planning.
10. Banking, trade and business and other services need – deregulation and liberalisation to accede to the EU
11. Human Rights and Governance Structures very weak
12. Police, Army and Judiciary need uniformity and not multi-layered too much ethnic focus.
13. We need a spirit of the Sarajevans from the siege days, to lift and unite us in one country/nation.
14. Many older citizens, I meet in cafes, shops and streets – said to me we need a new Tito who can unify the country and take us forward to the 21st century.

"The British Council in Sarajevo is performing a great service, with books, educational material and cultural information for young people "and must be fostered".

The Universities of Sarajevo and Colleges need to open up their ivory towers to the young and the less well off. Professors, some of Economics and Electronics are not geared up to the needs of globalisation.

The Education System must be geared up to the real needs of young Sarajevans, very keen to look forward to an E.U. contribution and to be part of a global modern society.

My enduring impressions of Sarajevo were very good and I feel, given peace and a safe and secure environment, the people of Sarajevo, young, middle aged and even old, will work together, without past rancour and 'hatred' which either due to religion or ethnic nationalism has been the bane of Sarajevo for several centuries.

Water fountain in Baasceraji, Sarajevo.

It should be an International City for all human-kind to grow and develop and flower as a bastion of multi-cultural/ multi-faith and universal ideals and aspirations as a bridge between East and West and central Europe.

Memories of Sarajevo, are precious to me not only the warm and friendly Sarajevans, but also some of its historic monuments – like the magnificent Old Town Hall/ national library built in the 16th century, burned by "Serb Criminals" in August 1992 (still not re-opened), the gregarious Bascarsija, Old Orthodox Church. The old Synagogue, The Roman Catholic Cathedral, The Great Gazi Hussef-Bays Mosque, The Tunnel under the Airport, the Olympic Stadium, Emperors Bridge, The Brotherhood and Unity Bridge, Mount Igman, the Snipers alley, The Place of the Assassination June 1914, Marshal Tito Barracks and the Jewish cemetery.

These 'Jewels' of Sarajevo city, tell us a story of pride and joy and sadness from the 16th century to today and that is the beauty and wonder of Sarajevo which is to me one of the most culturally integrated cities I have visited and enjoyed.

Some anthropologists and sociologists have tried to understand the mind set and aftermath of the Great Sarajevo siege of 1992-5 where over 49,000 people are alleged to have died including over 5000 children; Here are some anecdotal evidence of the "memory management" and transmitted memories of those dark and "Sarajevo Hiroshima" experiences[1]. "Hamida, Amara and Omar" are all Bosniacs (Muslim Bosnians) who lived in Sarajevo both before and during the 1991-5 war.

In 'socialist Sarajevo' the concept of the 'dobra stara porodics' (good old family) was an important one. Part of its significance lay in the characteristic Bosnian 'disdain' felt by urbanities for rural dwellers ("Primitive People"). Many Sarajevans whose parents had moved to the town from villages did not advertise this "image tarnishing fact" and during the 1991-5 war there was a urban tendency to blame the seljaci (villagers) combined with this urbanity, longevity implied the family in question somehow pre-dated Titoist socialism.

Amara – was always closer to the good, old family than Omar or Hamida who have blurred such distinction. This is in part because some of the previously gregarious families are perceived as having become over-associated with the corrupt political elites that emerged out of the 1991-5 war. It is also because old status distinction between Sarajevans have been challenged by the arrival of two new categories of Sarajevan residents. One the in-migrated Bosniac displaced persons (IDPs) from "ethnically cleansed villages" and a new wave of religious believers who have adopted Islamic values widely associated with some Arabs who participated in the war period (wahhabism). This new Wahhabism is experienced by many new Sarajevans, who embraced the old traditional 'dobra' (family) spectrum.

Hamida, Amara, and Omar are socially less distinct than they were before the war. All three have a certain threadbare status as people who remained in Sarajevo during the great siege. In the early days of the 91-95 war, they were considered brave and patriotic to remain in Sarajevo, as the war ground on, resentment for departing Bosniacs were tempered with understanding of their motives for leaving. By 2003, eight years after the siege was lifted, few Bosniacs claimed that, given the choice again they would stay in besieged Sarajevo.

In retrospect, staying is seen as having been pointless, and those who left returned with educational qualifications, language, skills and money, like several young people, I spoke to who had "run-away" to Switzerland, Germany, Italy and even England, now returned to the 'new Sarajevo'.

Amara is employed, Omar is self employed and Hamida has an employed dad. All three are linked to pre-war neighbourhood communities which offer support and have managed to build upon the remains of pre-war networks (Verze) which are now very important.

While aware that their situation is far better than the IDPs, people from this milieu are more consciously reminded of what they now have. Before the war, many were upwardly mobile. Regaining Economic ground lost in the war, is now seen as a challenge for the next generation.

Relative economic hardship (of returnees) is compounded by lasting sorrows of war – injury, bereavment, broken relationships (the divorced) of separated families and lost ambitions are still evident after the end of the war in 1995.

Serb artillery, History Museum, Sarajevo, 1993-96.

During the war, Sarajevo was encircled, sniped at, and shelled from the surrounding hills so that, as the Bosnian Serb military commander Ratko Mladic said "they can't sleep, so we drive them out of their minds". Like Omar, Amara, and Hamida, and others I meet in Sarajevo in July 2006 now live with the "Mladic legacy". This is a sociological process which the

Sarajevans who lived through the siege still face, whilst some of the IDP (returnees) do not share in that terrible nightmare.

I talked to two young people 24+ who said as boys of ten years old – they did not have eggs, milk or bananas, their mothers had to sustain them on pigeon-meat, and 'rotten bread' as flour was not available, yet they are now strong and brave men, looking to education and Europe for their new future, whilst the returnees did not suffer lack of food, but they too are in pain for what they lost during the war, as their families were fractured and some suffered loneliness and strange memories in other countries where they were refugees and educated.

The beauty of new Sarajevans, I noted is whether they stayed or left and returned, they have an over-riding desire to be better than in 1992-5 to educate, work and be successful in 2006 in the EU.

I shall discuss the prospects for Bosnia and Herzegovina's full accession to the EU in the future, in another chapter. Let me conclude my sojourn in the beautiful Sarajevo in July 2006 with a couple of anecdotes, I personally experienced there, that worry me for its future.

Museum and trams, Sarajevo, July 2006.

One – I took the infamous electric Sarajevo tram (some old from 19th century) from Bascarsija (opposite old Town Hall) to the Catholic cathedral only two stops round the corner on the Saturday before I left Sarajevo. I had only five Euros (nine Bosnian marks) and had to go to an ATM to get the currency to pay for my hotel (Hotel could not accept my Visa credit card as the system had collapsed).

The credit card facility at shops, hotels etc, are only 'status symbols' for modernity and the EU focus, not working or is dis-couraged by traders except at the Holiday Inn Hotel.

Anyway I had a ticket for the Tram, but not validated by punching for that journey (my ignorance or mistake). I was confronted by three conductors, who demanded a fine of KM 24.40 for a fare of KM 1.80 and they harassed and cajouled me to pay the fine inspite of me giving my last five Euro (9km). One very intimidating "mafia" looking Bosniac escorted me to the Turkish Bank ATM and the Volk Bank ATM in front of the Catholic Cathedral which woe-betide was not working even to get KM 50.

I then went into the Turkish Bank. five tellers and a manager were all women, not helpful and asked for my ID/Passport, which I had left in Emona Hotel for safety. They insisted on seeing it, which Adnan (Hotel Staff) was able to bring to the bank, after a frantic telephone call to Nejla (Manager) at Emona Hotel thank God for their kindness and help, but bank still would not give me the KM50 to pay the tram fine as my account was a Halifax Card one in the UK. By this time the "Mafiose Man" had left either thinking I was a CD (Diplomat) or a worse crook than them from abroad with some 'power' behind me.

Holiday Inn, Sarajevo, July 2006.

What is the morale of this story. Sadly the Bosnians are not ready to join the EU yet, their banking system and their electronics are poor and more so their tram system is antiquated and the staff are "petty hitlers". I was pleased in Sarajevo for the Emona Hotel Staff were so helpful to me and I am grateful to a small family owned hotel who made me safe and comfortable. Banks and Trams and Big Hotels I shall avoid in Sarajevo until they are less bureaucratic, 'mean minded' and aggressive as they are part of the establishment and live in the past.

Second and last anecdote , in Sarajevo Hotel Holiday Inn, one of the premier and well known hotels in city. I stayed the first three nights there, but was not comfortable or happy. Why? In spite of my Prority Club Gold booking from England.

It was a bad hotel, living in the glory of the 1991-5 war. Too old and still in the same mindset. Rooms were not modern with no Internet system, poor phones , electric plugs hanging from wall, and shower unit also hanging loose from bracket. Food was poor (except breakfast) and far too expensive, drinks were too dear, all lounges, reeked with cigarette smoke and uncleared ash trays. They had a NATO conference. 250 people in lounges, military, civilians and all sorts of arrogant people. The gym and pool was in the basement, antiquated from 1960s!

My friend and 'bodyguard' Mirza (Bell Boy, Holiday Inn Hotel),
and me at Emona Hotel, BentBaša.

In spite of all this it was tolerable, because I befriended an honest and friendly young Bosnian bell-boy called Mirza who resembled in size and appearance our 'hero' Freddy Flintoff of England and Lancashire. No relation or even a cricketer but who helped me as his "lost uncle" from England.

Nejla (Manager) and Edina, Emona Hotel –
Sarajevo, July 2006 – where I spent ten happy days.

The experience in the Holiday Inn was worse than the Trams/Banks incident in old city. Holiday Inn 4th floor where I had my room was next floor (5th floor) to the Italian wing – reserved for the visiting Defence minister and NATO/EUFOR General for the security conference held on 13th –14th July, for my bad luck when I was staying there. The whole place was guarded by crack Italian Carbeneri – not friendly, highly armed EUFOR troops in the outer perimeter of the Hotel. I felt safe with them, but not "secure" as the EUFOR motto is to provide Bosnia and Herzegovina with a "safe and secure environment" even now eleven years after Dayton accords which stopped the war.

The thing that 'killed' my empathy for the Sarajevo Holiday Inn hotel is the nasty and intimidating three plain clothed Italian body guards of the visiting Italian Minister of Defence who were armed with revolvers and hand-cuff equipment opposite my room – 4th floor, lift area, they were there day and night – two nasty men and a rude women – drinking coke, smoking and playing Suduko-crosswords to guard their VIP in 5th floor.

I felt my peace disturbed everytime I went in or came out of my room, which was near where they were watching their minister as civilian surveillance. I objected to the hotel manager who 'cared less' as EUFOR and conference was more important than a paid guest from England. So much for the 'war-minded' holiday inn in Sarajevo. It should be managed for the peace and prosperity and not re-live the siege and the snipers of 1992-5 which are long gone.

Melisa and her mother (Bascarsija Souvenir Shop). Melisa is studying hard at Sarajevo University and wanting to come to Cambridge, UK.

Jasmina, Master Cook at the Steak House Bascarsija.

In conclusion my short sojourn in Sarajevo was very good and beneficial. I left with hope for the young Sarajevans, but surprised by the amount of cigarettes, nice girls and strong young men who smoke a lot. They are ironically chain-smoking themselves to an early death of lung cancer and other respiratory diseases. Cigarettes are relatively cheaper there and have been available since 1890s a legacy of the Austro-Hungarian era, like coffee (black coffee) another addiction of all ages there (a legacy of

Ottoman Turk influence).The people of Sarajevo are great, but their
systems and administration are failing them.

To conclude this my dedication to the city of Sarajevo and her
brave people. Here are some sayings from others who suffered losses
in 1992-5 siege.

Curtesy

1. Anna Cataldi May 2000[2]

   "Voice of a besieged city" Letters from Sarajevo 1993-5.

   In loving memory of my son Giovanni who died tragically in August
   1993.

   Anna dedicates her book to every mother in Sarajevo, Moslem, Serb or
   Croat, with whom I now share the same irreplaceable loss"

   In my dreams I wander amongst the rubble in the old part of the city of
   Sarajevo – searching for a piece of stale bread.
   My mother and I breathe in the smoke from the dust of the shooting
   and imagine that it is the smell of cake and kebab.

"We run even though it is nine in the evening and perhaps were running
to meet "our" grenade then an explosion thunders through the street of
dignity, many people are wounded, sisters, brothers, mothers, and fathers. I

Damaged (1992) historic building – National Library, BentBaša.

move closer and touch an injured hand, I touch death, terrified I'm aware that it is not a dream, its just another day in Sarajevo."
Eding, twelve year old, Sarajevo 1993.

Roy Gutmen "Letters from Sarajevo" Foreward 1993.
'If Sarajevo were any other European capital, the assault on civilians by men with tanks and artillery from the safety of great distance (mountains) would be seen abroad as an intolerable atrocity". People would take to the streets in protest – at the siege which did not happen.

"Sarajevo is open to the world, it was a melting pot of cultures".

"The west had much to answer for in the unremitting siege of an almost 'undefended city'. Opting for the course of least resistance, its Governments (west) sent food and medicines but refused arms (UN arms embargo) for legitimate self-defence.

Thanks to Anna Cataldi (through UNICEF) in returning to Sarajevo again and again, the letters she collected from Sarajevans, conveyed the authentic unfiltered voice of Sarajevans. Sarajevans are citizens of the world – some letters convey a cry for help by those who curse their suffering – but others reveal the steel of their souls.

The burnt inside of National Library (August 1992), BentBaša.

"An astonishing number of Sarajevans would sooner die defending their city and its ideals than abandon it" Roy Gutman. With an epitaph to the Sarajevo siege and its brave and kind people, I would conclude this long chapter with two poignant letters curtesy of Anna Cataldi. "Letters from Sarajevo" 1994-5

Sarajevo 30th May 1992.
   "My dear Olga (Serb-Bosnian friend)
   It is truly dreadful that I should have to send you my sympathy like this on the death of your daughter. It hardly seems possible that times are such that our generation must bury its own children".

Muslim War Council, 1994-95.

I remember BentBa˘sa (old city) and our graduation ceremony. You invited me to your house afterwards for a cup of coffee. I pleaded a family engagement and said "I'll come some other time". Well this is "some other time" but did it really have to be so sad. I heard the news last night from my cousin, who was a friend of your daughters. I screamed. I have no idea if anyone heard my scream, it was something horrible, primitive. I can't believe that the "men" who come from elsewhere have no love for this city of ours. I cannot believe that on the very road to the Drveriza bridge that (see photos) that we used to walk along on our way to school, they should be killing our children as they go in search of bread with their poor little plastic bags.

Night after night I lie awake thinking, trying to imagine these creatures (I cannot call them men) who are shelling our city. Do you remember those times in our cellar when we shared our black bread with peanut butter and corn syrup with them? We were all equal.

Why did we ever allow them to come? Why did we allow them to study with us, graduate with us – without, however, absorbing our way of thinking and our tolerance?

For centuries Sarajevo has practised tolerance for which Latinluk, Talishan and Mahala are true metaphors.

I read that they are destroying everything. Can they destroy "everything" I do not believe.

I am more optimistic that when I spoke to Igor…. For all of you, too, who have remained in Sarajevo, choosing not to leave your native city.

My dear "anything I can say by way of consolation is probably useless". A pain such as yours is, they say the greatest one can experience far worse than the pain of childbirth".

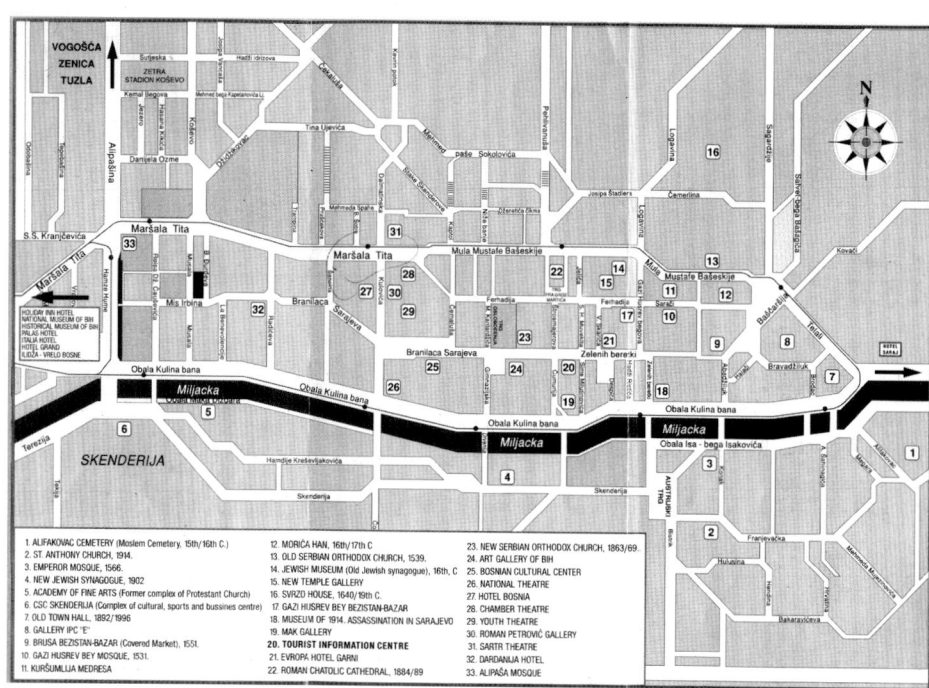

Map of Sarajevo.

The time will come when we can meet again, when we citizens of Sarajevo can once more look one another in the face of all that Andric * wrote about bells and clock towers, in spite of everything. I assure you of my love for you, and for all your family and my thoughts are constantly with you. Yours Merima (Bosnian Muslim friend).

This letter was written after the "Bread Queue Massacre" by a Moslem woman born in Sarajevo to her Bosnian friend whose young daughter was killed in Miskin Street (old city) on 27th May 1992.

Ivo Andric (1892-1975) winner of 1961 Nobel Prize for literature, born in Travaik and deeply pro-Serbian leanings.

Second letter out of over 80 letters smuggled in/out by Anna Cataldi.

2. Sarajevo – 2nd January 1993 (after a bleak cold new year).

Dear Cousins and Grandchildren

"An English journalist has offered to take this letter. He is going to Belgrade and told me that he would send it to you in Milan".

"Here everything is as it was. The cold continues to get worse and the shooting in the hill is relatively little, but you will know what I mean by relatively. We only receive one kilo of bread a week so I have tried to adapt the boiler and make an oven. But it needs firewood.

Your aunt who was such a robust woman, has shrunk to half her size and I am afraid the bombardment and all these horrors have driven her out of her mind.

When I leave home in the morning to go and look for firewood, she kneels in front of the door, and when I get back in the evening I find her in the same position. The nearest place for getting water is three kilometres away and one has to start queuing at dawn in order to have a hope of getting any so I am out for hours at a time. But what else can I do?

We are old, and even if we could get out of here, where would we go? How could we live? We no longer have any money and we cannot work, so what have we to hope for?

Sometimes when I go looking for wood, "I stayed hidden in the ruins for hours waiting for those who are younger and stronger than me to take what they want first, because I could not compete with them. Then I take whatever is left, and I remember that before this war started, I had a job and a respectable life and now I'm only an old man who has to rummage through the rubbish.

"Then I bless my sister for having given birth to two daughters who have made a life for themselves in Italy and are safe...."

Take great care of yourselves. A big hug,
Grandad Nermin.

References

1 Three Sarajevans and their social mileu – ref Cornelia Sorabji 2004.
2 Voice of a Beseiged City – Anne Cataldi – 'Letters from Sarajevo'
May 2000.

Multi-Faith, Sarajevo City

Emperor's (Careva) Mosque.

Catholic Cathedral.

Ascenah's Synagogue.

Orthadox Cathedral.

Chapter Eight

Srebrenica – The Truth and Justice

Pre-Massacre Period 1993-5 (Pre July 1995)

The tragedy of Srebrenica of 11th July 1995 to 15th July 1995 was such a calamitious event in the annals of modern Europe that Richard Holbrooke US under secretary under President Clinton called it as comparable to the Hitlerite/Nazi SS brutality of Katyn forest in Poland of 1940s.

To understand why it happened and how it was possible in the Balkans after the cold war in July 1995, is both easy and yet very poignant and difficult to rationalize about man's inhumanity to man.

I shall try to give some historically cultural and military reasons for this massacre of over 7100 Bosniacs (Muslim) at the hands of their once neighbours and compatriots – the Serb-Bosnians of Bosnia and Herzegovina.

First the historical perspective of Srebrenica. There were deep ancestral cleavages – traced back to 15th/16th century where the Ottoman Turks invaded a basically Slavic country.

The Ottoman Turks held sway for nearly four centuries in the Balkans converting many Slav – Christians both Catholic and Orthodox into Muslims. Some were given "janisnary status" in the Sultan's army and others were given land for services to the Pashas who had over all hegemony in the Balkans till the 20th century when the Austro-Hungarians repelled the Turks out of the Balkans. The Turkish influence was not only religious but cultural and a near one million pledged religious allegiance to the Ottomans. Thereby creating a 3rd force in Bosnia and Herzegovina.

Srebrenica was an Eastern border town not far from Serbia. The Drina River was a natural and sometimes hostile geographical boundary between Serbia and Bosnia but inter-marriage and ethnic tolerance and co-operation was prevalent in the eastern sector of Bosnia. The natural resources of Drina River Basin in which Srebrenica, Potocari and Bratunac were principal hubs, provided work and ample economic activity in the surrounding silver mines, and other metal factories. Under Marshal Tito during the 'glory' of the Yugoslava Federal Socialist Republic there was work in armaments and mining factories, Tito encouraged a rapid industrialisation process in Drina River valley and Basin areas. Srebrenica and Bratunac were in the 1970s thriving heartlands of both industrial and forestry activity. During this period under central socialist programs both Serb-Bosnians and Muslim Bosnians and even Croat – Bosnians worked in unity in-spite of their ethnic-religious diversity for the prosperity of Yugoslavia.

Srebrenica in the Pre-war census of 1990-91 recorded a population in excess of 32000 people about 56% Muslim Bosnian about 40% Serb-Bosnian and other diverse minorities, however in the 1940s (2nd World War) period, the demographic balance was a majority Serb-Bosnians.

The Muslim population increased rapidly in the 1970-1990 period with a higher birth rate, than that the slow growth of Serb-Bosnian communities. It is a sociological phenomenon difficult to explain, other than a biological one to say the Muslims were "breeding faster" in the 1980s, even when Tito died and Yugoslavia was fracturing.

It is cited by some Serb-Bosnian commanders especially General Mladic, who is alleged to have said, that the Muslim-Bosnians were breeding too fast, and he alluded to "Turkish dogs" in disdain of their breeding habits.

British Council material. Note General Mladic,(far right bottom)
still at large, October 2006. 'Srebrenica – record of a war crime'.

Ironically, the mini-explosion of Muslim Bosnians in Srebrenica and district, worried the Serb General and his political elites in the newly declared

Republika Sprska of a Serb autonomous entity, of which Srebrenica and district was a strategic corridor for the Serbs to their heartland in Banja-Luka and West Slavonia.

Srebrenica was not only rich in natural resources, but also strategically a natural land corridor for the Serbs to realise their dream of a historically strong Serb-dom from Belgrade to Banja Luka, where they felt Srebrenica and Drina River were part of their old heritage now inhabited by a Muslim majority.

There were clear strategic and cultural reasons why the Serb-Bosnian generals and Radovan Karadzic from Pale wished to control the Srebrenica and Drina river areas. There is clear evidence in the declarations of the strategic focus of Karadzic and General Mladic to ensure that Srebrenica and its hinterland should be under Serb control. This is strategy promulgated in 1992-3.

More so they convinced their Serb ethnic masters in Belgrade Milosevic and their co-partners the Catholic Croats in Zagreb under Tudjman, to carve up Bosnia and Herzegovina amongst the two larger states of Serbdom and Greater Croatia at the expense of the Muslim communities in BiH.

The above strategy did not take place due to the resistance of the Muslim Bosnians and the deal made later in 1992-3 by President Ailja Izebetgovic and his SDA party, with President Tudjman of Croatia to establish a Muslim-Croat Bosnian Federation to buttress the growing hegemony of the Republika Sprksa and its dream of greater Serbia.

All these background factors affected the fate of the Muslim Bosnians in Srebrenica Drina River District. The Serb forces inherited the overwhelming military assets from the JNA (Yugoslavia army) and personnel trained and dedicated to the historic dream and cultural animosity with their Muslim Bosnian neighbours.

In addition to these factors, Muslim forces whilst having had numerical superiority they were ill-equipped with pre- second world war equipment and old armour. The UN arms embargo was very harsh on the Muslim forces, who did not have the ability to re-equip their infantry and artillery with sophisticated weapons till later on in 1994 period.

In view of the Serb-Bosnian threat to Muslim enclaves the UNSC in 1993-4 declared six pre-dominantly Muslim areas as 'UN Safe Areas' – Gorazde, Bihac, Tuzla, Zepa, Srebrenica and Sarajevo were all designated safe areas under the protection of UNPROFOR.

In 1993-95 this resulted in calamitions consequences. UNPROFOR did not have a clear-cut mandate from UNSC in the early days, nor adequate resources of men and equipment nor mobile air support to really guard and save the Muslim populations in these havens.

The Serb-Bosnian High command knew of the UN predicament and weakness. Moreover they were enraged that the UNSC had declared five zones as safe areas – and not embraced the Serb minorities in these enclaves. It angered and precipitated Serb dislike for UN personnel who became hostages in Srebrenica and Zepa – the infamous 340 Dutch battalion (Dutch Bat) neither had the skill or ability to 'protect' the 18000-20000 Muslims in these 'safe areas' which were not safe in reality.

The Serb Generals insisted in negotiating a demilitarisation agreement with the Muslim forces and Dutch-Bat in 1993-4 for Srebrenica and Zepa, and having signed the de-militarisation agreement they abrogated it, and said they would protect the old and young of Srebrenica, as they knew the Dutch-Bat, had no military capability nor enough personnel to protect the Muslims there.

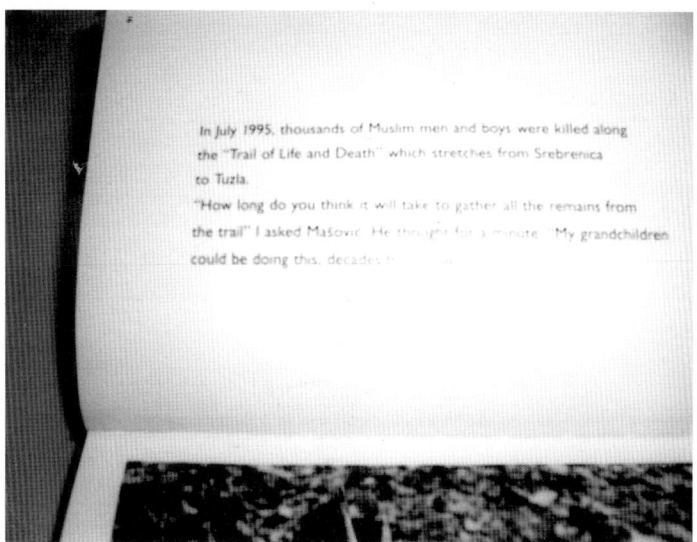

In July 1995, thousands of Muslim men and boys were killed along the "Trail of Life and Death" which stretches from Srebrenica to Tuzla.
"How long do you think it will take to gather all the remains from the trail" I asked Masovic. He thought for a minute. "My grandchildren could be doing this. decades "

British Council material – re Srebrencia tragedy..

In addition the Serb forces cut off food, medical supplies and other essential supplies to Srebrenica by controlling the access and bridges in the River Drina basin. Thus the Srebrenica population were dependent on the Serb forces both for humanitarian aid (supervised by UN/UNHCR) transfers in and out of Srebrenica and Zepa.

As the war intensified and the Serb forces suffered massive losses in Klin and Krajina areas further west at the hands of the now well-equipped and equally well led Croat forces, and NATO bombing of their artillery in Gorazde, frustrated and angry Serb-Bosnian military who wanted quick revenge on the UN 'safe' areas of Srebrenica and Zepa.

This Serb desire and military need was strategic to them in the broader annexation policy of at least 70% of Bosnia by 1993-5. They prepared for a massive assault on Srebrenica in the fall of 1993, and due to lack of full resistance of Muslim forces, and indecision of UNPROFOR the enclave fell into the hands of the Serb-Bosnian forces in early 1995.

In doing so, General Mladic wanted to neutralize the Muslim forces superiority in numbers of men and boys, from joining the resistance in Srebrenica and Zepa. There was a cold and calculated policy to isolate nearly 8000 men and boys of military age. 16-60 year olds and orders were given to deal with them, by first arresting them, and if they resisted to execute them on a mass killing basis.

Srebrenica t-shirt, courtesy of Mothers and Wives of Srebrenica and Zepa Safe Haven, and Bosnian Flag, courtesy of BiH Embassy, London.

The Bosnian Muslim High Command of the SDA was split between President Alija and his Prime Minister Sjaldjzic who failed to give unified orders to the ground commander of the Muslim armies in the Srebrenica and Zepa areas. Moreover Naser Oric and his brave, volunteer fighting force of some 1000-1500 were not under the command of the Eastern Muslim forces. There was confusion and no common tactical or even strategic focus to face the superiority of Serb-Bosnian forces.

It is felt that Naser Oric and other Muslim 'war-lords' tried independently to salvage a bad job and help protect their kith and kin in Srebrenica and Bruntanac.These clandestine Muslim forces also practised ethnic cleansing and "genocidal" policies against the Serb minorities in Tuzla, Bihac and even in Srebrenica, but what they did paled into insignificance by the Serb atrocities, in scale.

It is felt for Srebrenica people there were three "curses"
1. No real protection from UN Dutch Bat, in safe areas (illustration of map).
2. They were the majority there, but had been left weak and were not equipped to fight Serb-Bosnian on equal terms due to the UN Arms embargo.
3. Indecision of NATO, Contact group and US/UK vacillations on 'lift and stike' policy on Bosnia.

It is alleged in some text books and research material that in addition to the "3 curses" mentioned the people of Srebrenica were perhaps "sacrificial lambs" that President Alija "sold them down the river" – to get the Serb-Bosnian Generals to lift the siege on Sarajevo in 1994-5. This theory is plausible, but I believe is highly improbable as President Izetbegovic and the SDA, has had no such overt deal with the Serbs Bosnians in Sarajevo.

It is however a fact that according to my research militarily the Muslim Bosnian forces were not ready or adequately equipped to save Srebrenica, perhaps they "trusted" the UN too much, and by July 1995 according to General Michael Rose who retired in January 1995 and replaced by General Rupert Smith, had orders from the UNSC to withdraw UNPROFOR forces from Bosnia. This was a tragic and sad commentary at that time on UNSC's Bloc and Power politics and misguided action as we shall see in the next chapter (9) on the calamitions massacres of 11/7/1995-15/7/95 in Srebrenica and Potocari.

Chapter Nine

Srebrenica – Memories and Hopes
July 1995 to 2006

The horrendous massacres of Srebrenica, Potocari and Bruntanac district perpetrated by Serb-Bosnian forces between 11th July 1995 – August 1995 in the "Safe Area" were an affront to the civilized world.

Over 7100 men and boys of Muslim Bosnian ethnic extraction were killed by the occupying force of War Criminal General Ratko Mladic. The irony is that Mladic and his brutal murderers still say they came to "protect" the Muslim men, as the UNPROFOR Dutch Bat was neither equipped or mandated to provide them with real safety. Mladic used his 'God like' personality to charm, cheat and kill the Muslim men and boys of Srebrenica in a clear policy of blatant ethnic cleansing and genocidal behaviour comparable to the SS Generals of the Nazis of 1940s.

Potocari Memorial Building, opened 2005 by
President Clinton on the 10th Anniversay of Srebrenica.
(LA Digital Photos)

Mladics maniacal intention was not to emulate the Nazis who he hated, but to avenge for the Ottoman Turkish dominance of his Serb ancestors over four centuries ago. Mladic when he entered Srebrenica in 1995 in celebration said "Here we are on the anniversary of the famous rebellion of Dalijas of 1804 we shall avenge the wrongs that the "Turkish dogs" carried out on our ancestors. Mladic had a "God given" mission not only to avenge that battle of two centuries ago, but also to deliver Srebrenica and Drina River valley to his nation of a Greater Serbia, his ethno-nationalism was paranoidal. It is tragic that the UNPROFOR Generals including our own Sir Michael Rose fraternised with him and had lunch with him even in January 1995 when our General left the command of UNPROFOR[1]. General Mladic was indicted by the International War Crimes Tribunal in the Hague in Dec 1994, and it was a gross act of mis-calculation on the part of both UNPROFOR and NATO not to have arrested him, then Mladic is still at large as the UN and the west are still worried of arresting and bringing him to the Hague as they thought he could negotiate a 'just peace' in Bosnia and Herzegovina.

It is alleged that General Mladic is now suffering from cancer, and his wife and relations will surrender him if the West give them three million dollars as reparations. Mladic is said to be spending his "quiet retirement" in a farm in East Serbia where he has now 20 goats for his army and he has had the affront to call each one of his fat goats – after each of the UN Generals of UNPROFOR from 1991-1995 and other names of Western leaders and diplomats.

The mind boggels, at the thought every morning, Mladic calling his goats to a rosta – Lewis MacKenzie, Morilion, Michael Rose, Rupert Smith, John Major, Douglas Hurd, David Owen, Cyrus Vance, Akashi, Holbrooke and others, can you imagine his arrogance and his goaty vanity?

The five days of 11th July 1995 to 15th July 1995 is likened by Richard Holbrooke and other eminent writers, to a ghastly reminder of how cruel and brutal human beings like Mladic and Karadzic were, in their orders to execute over 7,109 Muslims, whose ancestors of the Turks over four centuries ago, and were perceived a treat to the realisation of the security of the Republika Sprksa and the Greater Serbian dream.

David Rohde of the Christian Science monitor more than any other writer, in his Pulitzer Prize winning book – End game "The betrayal and fall of Srebrenica" - Europe's worst massacre since World War 2" has admirably and graphically stated on a daily basis the gruesome and yet clinical genocidal action of the Serb forces under orders from General Mladic. I shall quote a few paragraphs, with his kind permission in this chapter to give you a graphic flavour of what happened in those dark days between 11th July and 15th July 1995, that shocked the civilized world, particularly the US, and the EU, into belated action which culminated in the Dayton Peace Accords in November 1995.

Potocari, old food factory warehouse, where thousands of
Muslim Bosnians were detained before execution, July 1995.

11th July 1995 "At 5.00 AM the sky began to glow to the east of Srebrenica. In the UN Dutch Bat compound, Captain Groen anxiously looked at his watch. Colonel Karremans (Dutch UN Commander) had told him that NATO planes would be circling over the Adriatic at 6.00 AM. All night Groen had worried constantly checking the time. The Serbs could have moved into the town at any moment. The shelling was endless, UNMO's counted 182 detonations during the previous night. The Serbs would have at least a full hour of light to move into town before NATO planes were in the air.

He thought that the enclave (UN safe area) would be saved. In the market place, Lieutenant Egberg ordered his driver to start the APC he and his men (peacekeepers) were edgy but optimistic. They were told NATO air strikes will come by 6.00 AM, which were relayed to the Bosnian and UN forces.

The eight men were afraid both of Muslim hand grenades and Serb shells, they had sealed their hatches while they rested. Trapped in the claustrophobic vehicle they listened as shells randomly careered into town. A mortar had landed ten feet from one of the APCs at 2.15 AM sending shrapnel pinging off the vehicles armour. Muslim soldiers had shouted "Fuck you" in English at them during the night. At dawn the Dutch peace keepers were happy to be still alive!!

"Prime Minister Haris Silajdzic of Bosnia in Sarajevo spoke to the town's (Srebrenica) leaders by radio, and he urged them not to harm or take any UN peacekeepers hostage!! The PM of Bosnia said the UN had assured him there would be NATO air strikes.

Egberg reached the area at 5.45 AM, he parked his APC in the trees where it could not be seen by the Serbs. A thick fog hung over the enclave. Srebrenica was eerily quiet. No artillery fire, no tank engines, no machine guns. The Muslim soldiers on the hill above them smiled and waved, to see the Dutch UN peacekeepers return.

At 6.00 AM Srebrenica's Major Fahrudin Saliowic and Muslim sector commander Ramiz Becivovic listened eagerly for sound of NATO jets streaking overhead. There was only a horrible empty silence!!

Egberg and his men were in position to guide the air strikes, but received no orders. In the Dutch compound of neighbouring Potocari, peacekeepers huddled in the bases bunker in case of retaliatory Serb shelling after the air strikes at 7.15 am, still no NATO planes!! at this anxious late hour, two white UN jeeps skidded to a halt in front of the post office. Two British commandos stormed the building.

They found Ramiz Becivovic and tried to tell him they needed a Muslim soldier who could point out the Serb positions. He couldn't understand them. Alma Hadzic the translator and Sanel Begic the Bosnian officer were confused. It was clear the Serb forces had not withdrawn from the enclave as the UN demanded.

"Why isn't it time for an air strike" – in broken English. The oldest Dutch peacekeeper said we (UN Dutch Bat) do not make the decisions. It is in Zagreb (capital of Croatia) where UN's Akashi and NATO commanders decide.

"Begic was furious, Ramiz Becivovic and the town leaders wanted to know where the NATO planes were. It was clear the Serb forces were preparing to attack the town. The Muslims had done exactly what the UN told them.... they were staying out of the "zone of death". It was found by 9.00 AM in Tuzla the Dutch chief of air operations was on vacation!! A Pakistani UN colonel acting for him said that, the 8.00 AM request for air attacks had been rejected because it was not on the proper format. The Dutch Bat had filed a request for Air Strikes, not close a air support form. They needed to be re-submitted, with an updated target. The Dutch lieutenant in town was furious, more than one hour had been lost.

By 9.45 AM Tuzla re-submitted the request to Sarajevo UN and then again, as it did not have a proper targeting list that indicated Serb positions to the north and south of the enclave. This was not only the height of bureaucracy but a matter of life and death, the Muslims of Srebrenica were sacrificed to the gross UN/NATO red-tape.

The irony of it all was as David Rohde says, due to all this bungling red tape, the NATO's planes which were scrambed early morning had returned to bases in Italy, short of fuel over the Adriatic.

Luckshan Abeysuriya on the way to Srebrenica,
15/7/06, in Republika Sprska (Serb-Bosnian entity).

Thus close air support was not available on 11th July 1995. The Post Office radioed and ordered Hadzic and Begic to leave. There would be no air strike. "Enraged Begic was convinced that Srebrenica was being sacrificed. He radioed his field commander Ramiz Becivovic with the question about the Dutch and British in front of him... Can I kill them, he asked?

David Rohde says further the mayor Fahrudin Salihovic and others decided that their town had been intentionally sacrificed by their Bosnian Government and the UN.

"Under pressure from the US, UK and France, the Bosnian Government had agreed to the much rumoured secret deal with the Serbs. He was convinced Srebrenica was being traded for one of the suburbs surrounding Sarajevo that was controlled by the Serbs. Salihovic thought the Sarajevo siege would end, with a land link given by the Serbs, but Srebrenica was the price.

This conspiracy theory had been contested by the 1995 Muslim Government in Sarajevo. I failed to get an answer in even 2006 from the Bosnian embassy here in London who instead blamed NATO and UN and of course the weak and ineffective Dutch Bat in the Drina River valley.

The great irony, according to David Rohde – p.p. 148 – the end game is that General Janvier (NATO) and the Japanese UN diplomat Akashi signed the request for close air support, which General Mladic did not understand nor believe was a threat, as it was five days after the original Dutch bat request – NATO had confused the UN peace -keepers with a technical difference between CAS (close air support) and full air strikes, the latter which the Serbs feared.

There were some weak air strikes by NATO – without the right laser-guided bombs, the Serb force radioed Potocari "If the NATO attacks do not stop, immediately all Dutch peacekeepers in Serb custody will be killed"....... the Dutch compound in Potocari where 1000s of Muslim civilians are gathering, will also be shelled. This was a serious Serb ultimatum.

Panic set in Potocari and Srebrenica by mid-day, thousands of old, women and children and Dutch peace keepers slowly streamed north in a fierce July sun.

By 4.15pm on 11th July 1995, soldiers from the Bosnian Serb Army entered the Dutch UN compound in Srebrenica town, they encountered no resistance from the Dutch and almost none from the Bosnians who had no overall commander since the feared Nasir Oric was withdrawn from there.

The world's first UN Safe Area had fallen, only one Dutch peacekeeper and about 75 Muslim soldiers died defending the safe area. In the most stunning victory of the war, approximately 50-75 Serb soldiers died conquering it. General Ratko Mladic triumphantly entered Srebrenica where he gave an interview to Serb TV. "Here we are in Srebrenica on July 11th 1995, on the eve of yet another great Serb holiday". We present this city to the Serbian people as a gift. Finally, he said after the great rebellion of the Dalizas the time has come to take revenge on the Turks in this region.

The Serb General was referring to the Serb uprising that the Turks brutally crushed in 1804. Over 190 years later, Mladic was looking for revenge. Thousands of Muslim refugees, women carrying children filled the road from Srebrenica, while a few light blue helmeted UN Dutch troops with white UN APCs dotted the crowd.

Fresh wreaths and flowers for the 11th anniversary
of Srebrenica Tragedy at Potocari. 15/7/06.

This was a humanitarian catastrophy which the UN/NATO could have stopped with a clear strategy and firm decision but was full of red tape and vacillation of the UNSC and EU leaders.

Recently in 2003, Kofi Annan was asked by the Mothers Association for victims of Srebrenica and Zepa. Why the UN did not save their husbands and sons? Kofi shamefaced answered "the UN made mistakes". It was a pathetic response from the UN Secretary General.

I was in Potocari and Srebrenica, eleven years after the massacres in 15th July 2006, I was used to death and tragedy in Sri Lanka, Cyprus, Nepal and Belfast with my work for Human Rights, but I could hardly contain my pain, remorse and tears accompanied by my young driver and guide.

When I visited the historic Potacari memorial where a great marble white wall shows the names, date of birth and date of death of the 7109 massacred by the Serb forces. All these names are human beings, husbands, brothers, sons, and grand sons between 16-60 years of age who the Serbs systematically slaughtered in a bloodbath between 11/7/1995 and August 1995.

Luckshan Abeysuriya at Potocari Memorial, July 2006.

My worst trauma was to see the thousands of graves in Potocari as far as the eye can see, some fresh, only re-buried with Muslim funerals – some 550 remains laid to rest only on 11/7/2006, only four days before my visit, the flowers and soil of the burial mounds were still fresh. It was the most poignant sight I have seen in my 70 year life.

My young driver and I were in tears, sharing with other relatives there the grief and shock eleven years after the tragedy, we felt the dead are now remembered and those buried after Muslim funerals were finally at rest, but there are still searches for thousands of missing remains which the ICMP (International Commission for Missing Persons) in Bosnia and the Mothers Association for Srebrenica and Zepa victims are digging some 'mass graves' which the Serbs hid and desecrated in the Drina River basin in 1995.

We proceeded to Srebrenica town and to my surprise and horror was it was like a ghost town, still damaged and with some returnees but still after eleven years looking forlorn and lost. To my driver and me, it was a tragic view (see photos in book) and we returned too emotionally upset to the comfort of Sarajevo and the warmth in my Hotel Emona. That day I shall not

Above and below: Srebrenica main street, deserted. July 2006.

forget and in a sense I felt I was there sharing the grief for the victims, survivors and for the United Nations of which I am a great supporter in England.

On 21st July 2006 after arranging an interview on the telephone with the ladies of the movement of mothers from Srebrenica and Zepa – in Antuna Hangijza Sarajevo; I went with an educated young lady, Senita Delibasic, as my interpreter/guide to meet two mothers, in the heat of Sarajevo, after a good lunch near UNITIC tower. The steak house run by a Bosnian Enterpreneur which served excellent fare.

I was introduced by my guide as a researcher from England, who hopes to write a book on the Srebrenica tragedy and its aftermath. The two ladies, Sabra and Suada were very angry with the UN, International Community, their Government and generally still full of sorrow, at their tragic losses. The initial re-action to me, coming from England was not friendly, as the widows said Britain both the UN generals here, and the then John Major Government did not do enough to save Srebrenica nor they have helped much to share in their search for victims and remains. President Clinton and his sad pensive photograph decorated the office, and I was able to refer to Bill Clinton who at Dayton and later was a friend of the Muslim people, but the mothers felt he was too late in acting to stop the Serbs.

The two mothers said in Bosniac, interpreted by my friend Senita that the west failed to protect the Muslims and that the Serbs were allowed to take the "law unto their hands" there was no respect for Human Rights or Humanitarian law, it was pure genocidal practice.

The mothers said "The Bosnian Muslim government too had failed the survivors of Srebrenica and Drina River valley people. In 1995 there was no concerted government policy to protect them even the UN was too weak and full of red tape.

Since the tragedy, there is universal revulsion and empathy, but still some International agencies except perhaps the ICMP, and UNHCR, are not helping the mothers and widows to seek help to adequately fund their programmes to re-bury the remains (bones and other remains) and to find adequate burial grounds in that area which is under the Republika Sprksa, is a situation full of problems and bureaucracy.

The mothers I spoke to gave me graphic postcards of items of clothing of the victims, and a very poignant set of postcards for justice, which I treasured, and are exhibited in the book as a dedication to those people's devotion to their dead and missing relatives.

I would like to conclude this chapter with some extracts from the booklets 2002-2003 'Akivnosh' published by the Mothers from Srebrenica and Zepa enclaves (curtesy of UNDP Sarajevo Press Office) – as a poignant appendix –

1. "Mothers' letter to son 2001"
2. "Exhibition Yr 2000 (pages 27, 28, 29)"
3. "Where further to go"

Finally the movement of mothers of Srebrenica and Zepa Enclaves gave me a new Tee-shirt – graphically stating 'Do not forget – the genocidal action in

11/7/1995' which I shall proudly wear in UK to promote their noble work. (Photo in book of me wearing tee-shirt at Grange with my cat Sampras).

Reference
1 "Fighting for Peace" – Sir Michael Rose, 2000

Potocari, new graves, July 2006.

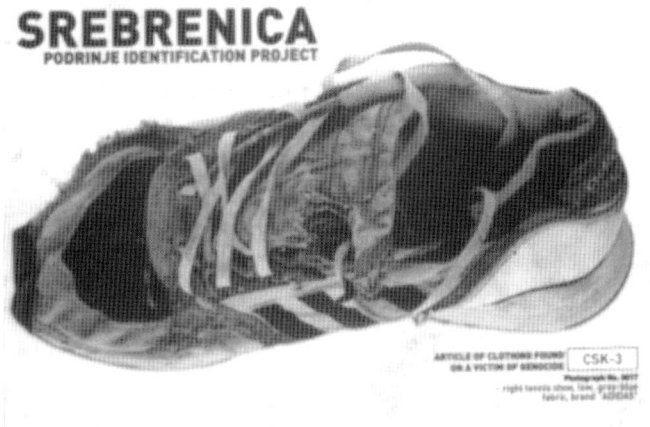

Postcard for Justice.

Mother's letter

My dear son,

Your mother is writing you a letter, although I have never received an answer to the letters I have written, because I have always sent them to an unknown address. It has been like this for five years; on 11 July 2000 it will be five years since we were separated. And I will never forget that day. Serb soldiers took you away from me in front of the blue helmets in the UN safe haven of Srebrenica.

I have been waiting for you for five years, and I hope that you will come back to me alive, and I am thinking of the way I'm going to feel that day, for I will never accept that you are dead. Serb soldiers took you away before the international community's very eyes, and I have every right to request from the international community to bring you back to me. And not only you, but all the people that Serb soldiers took away with them, and it is a large number (10.701) of men. They are all somebody's sons. All the mothers are searching for the truth about their missing children.

Serb soldiers took you away from me, and your two brothers and your father, who started their journey through the woods, have not come back either. For five years I have been living alone and waiting for you to come back. Forgive me, but I have no more tears to shed, because they have dried up, and I do not know how much longer I will have to wait.

I will never forgive the world leaders who let this evil happen to me and other mothers, and who did nothing to prevent it.

I have asked, and I will continue asking the international community to give me an answer WHY my beloved ones are gone, how much longer I will have to wait and live alone? Believe me, my son, the life I am living is no life at all.

Please, answer me if you get this letter, and come to your mother who is longing for you.

Your mother

Courtesy of Association of Citizens Movement,
Mothers andWives of Srebrenica and Zepo Enclaves.

Exhibtion

It is important to say a few words about the exhibition organized by the Mothers of Srebrenica and Zepa Enclaves. Members of the organization worked hard for months prior to the exhibition so as to be able to present their best work to the important guests. The exhibition showed the great skill of Bosnian women, from carpet weaving to embroidery. However, the exhibition itself, held on the premises of the International Committee of the Red Cross, meant much more to the Mothers of the Srebrenica and Zepa Enclaves, for representatives of the international community spoke publicaly for the first time about the crime.

Petritsch: OHR, Year 2000

Women of Srebrenica, ladies and gentelmen, we are here to mark a dark day. On 11 July, 1995, Srebrenica fell to Bosnian Serb forces. Women, children and the elderly were forced onto buses and expelled. They did not know - and still don't know today - what happened to their husbands, sons, fathers and brothers; men and boys who tried to escape through the forests and mountains of eastern Bosnia, the land where they were born.

I find it difficult to even begin too comprehend how civilised life could have broken down in such a brutal and terrifying way.

I find it difficult to even begin to meet adequately their families' sorrow - especially those who are with us tonight. The **true figure is not 7,412 missing – it is tens of thousands of wives, daughters, mothers and sisters who still hurt from the evil done in Srebrenica.**

Judge Riad, of the war crimes tribunal in The Hague, spoke well when he described the acts of those who ordered and committed this unspeakable crime as: "truly scenes from hell, written on the darkest pages of human history".

As a representative of the international community, I am also fully aware of how we failed the people of Srebrenica that day. A "safe haven" was anything but safe. This day shamed the international community. We have a

lasting obligation to continue to help the people of
Srebrenica Bosnia and Herzegovina.

Tonight's gathering is a hopelessly small and symbolic gesture.
Along with coming to terms with what happened, the women of
Srebrenica must still struggle to make a living five years on.

The crime of Srebrenica must never be forgotten. It is a
disgrace that five years later there is no decision on a location
for a cemetery and memorial to the dead and missing.

I would like to offer international expert advice to help come
up with a plan for a memorial site. This advice is offered
alongside the work already undertaken by the joint
Bonsiak/Serb Commission on the site in Srebrenica. I also offer
my authority to help in any way I can to make sure such a site
is established as early as possible. The memorial would not only
be for the dead and missing. (The memorial must enable the
families left behind to grieve). The memorial must serve to
tell all in Bosnia and Herzegovina – never again.

But I also put it to you that the most lasting justice for
the victims of Srebrenica would be the return of Bosniaks—
the victims' families – to their homes in Srebrenica. This is
already underway. I will do all in my power to make sure
return to Srebrenica continue and that people are able to
rebuild their lives.

Return is at the heart of Dayton. Return is at the heart of
placing a tolerant and multi-cultural Bosnia and Herzegovina
in Europe.

Return will not undo this terrible massacre, but return would
show that the authors of ethnic cleansing did not achieve their
criminal goal. And I voice a timid hope - difficult at this time
for you - that by marking this day, we will all of us move
forward along the difficult path of reconciliation. Only along
this path can we truly declare - never again.

Thank you.

The President of the Association used this opportunity to invite
ambassadors and the highest representatives of the local and international
institutions to support them in their search for the truth:

Munira:

"I invite everyone present to pay tribute, with a minute's silence, to our poeple who were taken away or were captured and remain unaccounted for.

I would lke to thank all of you on behalf of the co-ordination board for having accepted our invitation to this exhibition of handicrafts made by the members of the Association, who are dealing with tracing the missing persons from the UN 'safe haven' of Srebrenica.

You are invited today to show, by your presence, that you are aware of the enormous tragedy of Srebrenica, that you know what happened there, and to see that the families of the missing sons, brothers, fathers and husbands are still here, waiting for answers about the fate of their loved ones.

For us, the families of the missing, the prority is to find out the truth, however painful it may be; to bury the dead in a dignified way, and to try to pick up the pieces of our broken lives.

The majority of the families are left without their breadwinners, and many of us are without our underage children. Our lives are difficult, and the only thing that can bring relief is information about our missing family members.

We appeal to all of you to do your utmost and use your position and power to help the families obtain information about their loved ones. Do everything you can to ensure compliance with the Dayton Agreement, espcially the part which states that the Parties commit themselves to exchange information on the missing.

Help us, help those who are stilll alive to find out where our children's bones are, give us a chance to bury the dead in a dignified way! Help us even if you could not help them!

I would like to thank the International Committee of the Red Cross, the Office of the High Representative, and the International Commission for Missing Persons, and to invite all of you to come with us, the mothers, to the place from where our loved ones were expelled in 1995."

Where further to go?

Theoretically, to give an answer to this question is very easy - to find the missing, to identify the bodies, and then to bring back both the dead and alive to Podrinje. In practice this process, which everyone who has some possibility to exercise power subscribes to, is going to last for a long time. For how long will it last, no one dares to estimate, but... there are certain indicators that are obvious.

Under optimal conditions, the identification of those bodies for whom this is possible will take seven to ten years. It is difficult to say how long the search process will take. At a meeting between Amor Masovic, head of the Federal Commission for Tracing the Missing, and representatives of nine family associations of the Missing, certain problems that are occurring in this process were mentioned, such as the limitations of the competent institutions, financial difficulties, and lack of cooperation.

If the problems that those who are alive are faced with are added to this, apart from the eviction issue, it is clear that the process of return will also be long-lasting and slow. A slight increase in the number of returnees to Srebrenica during the last year was just an indication of the process which could gather momentum once the truth about what was happening in Srebrenica is revealed. One part of the truth was highlighted during the legal proceedings against a General in the Army of the Republika Srpska, Radislav Krstic, at the Hague Tribunal. However, this is but one of the links in a long chain of those who have to be finally punished. The punishment should also include persons committing arson against returnees' homes, or those who stoned buses full of women who wanted to say a simple prayer for their dead, or those who discriminated against the non-Serbian population. There are many examples of this. The aforesaid peaceful assemblies of Srebrenica survivors on each 11 July, can be considered as a kind of contribution to the fight for human rights.

Courtesy of Association of Citizens Movement,
Mothers andWives of Srebrenica and Zepo Enclaves.

ARTICLE OF CLOTHING FOUND ON A VICTIM OF GENOCIDE   LZ-2B-39
Photograph No. 1609
- blue jeans, brand "CARRERA"

SREBRENICA
PODRINJE IDENTIFICATION PROJECT

ARTICLE OF CLOTHING FOUND ON A VICTIM OF GENOCIDE   CSK-31
Photograph No. 0161
- denim jacket, light blue, brand "LEVI'S"

SREBRENICA
PODRINJE IDENTIFICATION PROJECT

Sauda (mother) and Senita Delibasic (my interpreter).

Sauda (mother) and Author after Interview, Sarajevo 21/7/06.

Chapter Ten

The International Criminal Tribunal for Former Yugoslavia

The United Nations Security Council, established the ICTFY in late 1993, to enable it to indict the war criminals of former Yugoslavia.

Its first Prosecutor was the well known South African Jurist Richard Goldstone, he was of the view that it is essential for peace and reconciliation that the principal actors of genocidal behaviour Milosevic, Kardazic, General Mladic, and several other lesser known Croat, Serb and Muslim Bosnian war criminals should be tried and sentenced as soon as the due processes of law and justice allowed.

However nearly twelve years later we are still struggling to mete out justice to two of the principal culprits who were more than anybody was accused of the Srebrenica massacres of 1995. Karadzic and Mladic had not been arrested. Even though a massive 'search' has taken place to locate them and bring them to trial.

It is my belief, that both Karadzic and General Mladic are well protected by Serbia and an arrest by NATO/EUFOR even today (August 2006) could result in some ethnic disturbances particularly in Bosnia and Herzegovina and large scale protest in Belgrade.

The tribunal has spent several years on the infamous Slobodan Milosevic trial in the Hague, with the current Chief Prosecutor personally facing the late Serb Dictator to speed up his punishment. It is both tragic and an affront to International Justice, that instead of justice being meted out, the principal accused died in detention in the Hague of natural causes. There was some speculation, in Serbia and in the Republika Sprska that Milosevic had been "poisoned" and his death was designed as an insult to the way the tribunal carried out its trial.

Carla Del Ponti - the current Prosecutor, has served long and hard, trying to mete out justice, for nearly twelve years for the people of Bosnia, in particular the survivors of Srebrenica and other areas – who are waiting for the final trial of General Mladic and Radovan Karadzic. Instead of "grabbing the bull by its horns" Ponti and her co-prosecutors, are 'playing a waiting game' in the hope that both Mladic and Karadicz will perhaps die of natural causes like their guru and henchman Milosevic.

Justice must be meted out fairly and quickly in a country like Bosnia, and it is no good hiding behind an ineffective and indecisive NATO/EUFOR which are vested with the role of providing a "safe and secure environment" in Bosnia. Bosnia is crying out for justice to put behind bars the two men who ordered the massacres in Srebrenica. The longer this is not done, the pain, the trauma and anger of the Bosnian Muslims will fester, and affect not only Serbia, but also the chances of Bosnia acceding to the EU.

Admittedly the ICTFY have sentenced lesser war lords like Nasir Oric and others, but it is legal lunacy to leave the two principal perpetrators of genocide and ethnic cleansing at large, in a country where justice must be meted out sooner rather than later.

There is of course a pending trial in the ICJ (International Court of Justice) between the state of Bosnia and Herzegovina which will bring a fellow state Serbia to the court on a charge of genocide, which was heard in non-summary proceeding in November 2005, now judgement is expected in 2010 at least.

The UN must speed up the due process of law and justice in the Hague, both in the ICTFY and ICJ to bring home justice to the millions of Bosnian Muslims now living with tragic memories in 1993-95.

The recent controversial judgement in June 2006 of Naser Oric, 39 years old Bosnian Muslim military commander (war lord) at Srebrenica, his conviction was of a term of only two years in prison for the indictment for failing to prevent the torture and murder of Serb-Bosnian prisoners in 1993. Oric was cleared of further charges, of direct involvement in the atrocities of destruction of Serb-Bosnian villages.

His punishment of two years in prison was welcomed naturally in Sarajevo, but was sharply criticised in Banja Luka (capital of Republika Sprska) Serb and Serb-Bosnian leaders said the decision reflected dual standards and undermined the ICTY's credibility. The Serbian President Boris Tadic called the sentence "scandalous" as their Prosecutors had asked for an 18 year term!

I believe, the whole administration of justice system of war criminals in former Yugoslavia is a mess with a number of Tribunals, Courts and Jurisdictions having an ineffective due process of law. This not only undermines the credibility of the UN and the judicial system of both Serbia and Bosnia and to a lesser extent Croatia. My considered view is the ICTFY should be given an UNSC ultimatum of say another twelve months before the Prosecutor in charge Ponti, should terminate the tribunal, there is very little confidence in it, twelve years after Srebrenica, when the two principal perpetrators are still at large, it is a sorry commentary on the Bloc politics of the United Nations Security Council and North Atlantic Treaty Organisation's vacillation, for fear of Serbia's reprisals in Kosovo.

The question of genocide and adequate compensation for the Bosnian victims survivors like the mothers/widows of those who perished in Srebrenica and Zepa and other areas in 1993-5 should be dealt by the ICT and justice should be speeded up against Serbia and its correspondents in Bosnia.

This is not only a pre-condition for successful accession talks of Bosnia and Serbia to the EU, but more importantly natural justice and International law must be adhered to for survivors of Srebrenica, to enable them to lay at peace their current pain.

Karadzic and Mladic indictments of the ICTFY are complex and long-winded, and even if both are arrested tomorrow and committed personally to trial, it will take months for the complex and "bureaucratic" processes of the tribunal to come a conclusion. Ironically the UN and the International legal processes here are a burden on Natural Justice in Bosnia and Herzegovina.

Radovan Karadzic founder member and President of the Serbian Democratic Party (SDs) until 15th July 1996, became President of the National security council of the so called "Serbian Republic of Bosnia and Herzegovina on 27th March 1992, and became President of the three member Presidency of the Serbian Republic on 12 May 1992. He was a member of the Supreme Command of the armed forces of the Serb-Bosnian republic from on or about the 30th November 1992; sole President of the present Republika Sparksa and supreme commander of the armed forces from 17th December 1992.

Karadzic is a doctor/ psychiatric specialist who is now alleged to live in a health farm in Slovenia under guard by his 'Serb henchmen'.

The ICTFY indicted him for genocide, complicity in genocide, extermination, murder, wilful killing, persecutions, deportations, inhuman acts, unlawfully inflicting terror upon Muslim civilians, and taking of hostages, it is indeed a formidable charge sheet from 1995. He is charged with on the basis of individual criminal responsibility (Article 7(1) and superior criminal responsibility for massacres carried out by Serb-Bosnian forces in Srebrenica during period 15th July 1995 to August 1995 (amended indictment November 2002).

This vile and cunning theoritician and "medical maniac" is still at large, avoiding the NATO forces of EUFOR in Bosnia and Herzegovina. General Ratko Mladic, the twin force of evil of the Bosnian Serbs – Commander of the Bosnian Serb Army, and his high command of the BSA, developed a plan to murder the hundreds/thousands of Muslim men in Potocari. The large scale systematic murder of Muslim men and boys from Srebrenica which began on the morning of 13th July 1995 continued through July and August.

At the same time as the killings and mass graves carried out by General Mladic's men, the BSA and Serb police forces transported thousands of Bosnian women, children and elderly men out of the area. This was a deliberate act of ethnic cleansing, and also systematic rape of Muslim girls and older women which was as an act of war, now and is a crime against humanity. The Serb forces wanted to create a new community in the Drina River basin of Serb fathered babies and criminals born of raped Muslim defenceless women. This was not only contrary to International law provisions of the new International Criminal Court – Rome Statute of 2000, but also an affront to Muslim/Turk sensitivities and cultural identity.

General Mladic had personally supervised the attack on Srebrenica, was responsible for the horrendous murders of over 7109 (ICRC numbers) of ethnic Muslims as a direct revenge for the actions of their Turkish ancestors of four centuries ago. The perpetrators were blessed by Serb orthodox priests as they carried out the carnage.

The continued and deliberate in-action of EUFOR who is mandated to "search and seek out" PIFWCs (persons indicted for war crimes) to justice. Even as recently as 13th July 2006, the current EUFOR Italian Major General Marco Chiarini, who met Carla Del Ponte, Chief Prosecutor of ICTFY in Sarajevo airport HQ, the General pledged support for the speedy 'arrest' of the PIFWC's principals Karadzic and Mladic who are avoiding NATO/EUFOR.

The complex Dayton Peace accord, structures of the OHR (Office of High Representative) and dysfunctional legal and administration of the framework agreements of Dayton are preventing both EUFOR/NATO and the ICTFY, concluding their work in bringing the principal perpetrators to justice speedily there and the lack of will of the UNSC to back the ICTFY's work. This is an added factor for the current UNs low esteem in Bosnia and Herzegovina, where the Muslim people are crying out for natural justice.

I leave with you, the great disappointment felt by Bosnian Muslims having visited Bosnia and Herzegovina in July 2006, that the NATO/EUFOR personnel have not yet delivered Messers Karadzic and General Mladic to the ICTFY, I quote Carla del Pontes famous words – to the Time magazine in March2006". "Ratko Mladic is in Serbia, there is no doubt about this. He has been there since 1998. During all this time he has been… within reach of the Serbian authorities in Belgrade". He can and must be arrested immediately". This was the chief Prosecutor's folorn plea to the Serbian Government and to the International Community still unheeded! What an affront to International Justice.

Even on 27th March 2006, when Sloboden Milosevic was finally laid to rest in Belgrade, the ICTFY urged the Serb President to hand over Milosevics hencemen to the Hague tribunal, but up to July 2006 attempts by NATO forces and Serb Police have led to frustrations. European Union foreign ministers have urged Serb authorities to hand over Karadicz and Mladic to the Hague tribunal even in March 2006. It was stated until this is achieved the long delayed accession to the EU, talks for Serbia and even Bosnia and Herzegovina are being affected.

Here we are in July 2006, when I was in Bosnia, still EUFOR/NATO personnel are not delivering the two Arch War Criminals to the Hague. Ironically, Milosevics death in custody at the Hague, has fanned ugly nationalist sentiment and increased fears among Serb officials that arresting Mladic now would produce a violent backlash that could threaten Serb government stability. A distraught Serb official said to the Time magazine in March 2006. "There was a time when we could have arrested Mladic, but we did not, now we want to but we cannot".

Karadic (no relation to Radovan) – a Serb rights investigator is very sceptical, he told the Time magazine – "Serbia may never hand over Mladic, since his testimony in the ICTFY may confirm Serb guilt for war crimes in Bosnia". Another Serb, Draskovic, who escaped two assassination attempts during Milosevic's time in power says "he is unimpressed by the efforts of the Serb security services "Either they are protecting General Mladic or they are incompetent".

Chapter Eleven

The Dayton Accords – 1995

The Dayton Peace Accords were agreed in November 1995 and signed in Paris in December 1995, to officially end the Balkans wars of 1991-95.

Much of the credit to the run up to and signing of Dayton Accords is due to the unremitting efforts of US under-secretary Richard Holbrooke, personal envoy for Bosnia of President Clinton. Holbrooke, in his excellent book "How to end a war" very vividly explained the daily efforts for a cease fire and eventual peace in Bosnia. It is riveting reading.

I only wish Clinton and Holbrooke and perhaps Warren Christopher – Secretary of State and later on Madeline Albright, started their "odyssey for peace", 18 months earlier. The US and EU contact group and Russia, if they had showed the same commitment after August/September 1995 to ending the war, then the Srebrenica massacres may not have happened in July 1995.

In a strange and bizarre way, the massacre of 7109 Muslim men and boys precipitated Dayton, as it shocked the US, the EU, and the UN to belated action. The legacy of the Sarajevo siege and the tragedy of Srebrenica is still in the consciousness of us who are now trying for peace, development, justice and security through the Dayton Accords.

I applaud "Holbrooke, Carl Bildt and Ivanov" talks preceding Dayton, which prepared the ground for President Bill Clinton to "bang the heads" together of Milosevic/ Tudjeman and Izetbegovic the three Presidents of the warring states. At Dayton Ohio, the US cleverly master minded the peace negotiated by tough and uncompromising zeal to get the three warring Presidents, to agree to a cease-fire on 5th October (at Geneva) and then in November to sign the accords.

I shall explain in some detail the Dayton framework accords its strengths, weakness, principal institutions and current tensions, later in this chapter, but let me give my readers, some valuable concepts behind the Dayton accord and how the US/EU/UN finally brought to an end a most vicious and damaging ethnic war in Bosnia and Herzegovina which led to nearly 200,000 deaths including over 7100 in one week in July 1995 in Srebrenica. Over one million of the five million people of Bosnia displaced, including over 6000 children dead, or missing.

By August/September 1995, the world was aghast with the Bosnian Imbroglio. It not only shocked the outside world but the three principal combatants. The Serb dictator Milosevic and his clients in Serb-Bosnia – Republika Sprksa had achieved a chilling expansion of land and terriotory of Bosnia and Herzegovina – some 42% of its terriotory, for 35% of the ethnic mix, even though they liked more land (in 1993-4) they occupied nearly 70% of Bosnia, with their superior JNA, fire power and help from Serbia. During early 1994-5, the Serb-Bosnians suffered great damage at the hands of Tudjuman's Croat military superiority re-inforced by both German and US (unofficial) military advise and armaments. The UN arms embargo imposed by the UNSC in 1991, was both weak and ineffective, as far as the Croats were concerned who openly flouted it, even Belgrade was able to circumvent the arms embargo, in any case the Serb-Bosnians inherited or commandeered the bulk of the military assets of the defunct Yugoslavian National/Peoples army of Marshal Tito. It was the Muslim Bosnians who suffered most in 1992-5, by the iniquity of the UN arms embargo, which eventually they breached in 1994, to re-equip and re-vitalise the Bosnian Muslim battalions with help of funds and arms from fellow Muslim countries, principally Iran and Saudi Arabia. It was alleged that President Aliza Izetbegovic entertained in be-sieged Sarajevo, to frugal dinner some Bin Laden emissaries and that he gave 500 Bosnian passports to Muslim mercenaries from Afghanistan. This is now strongly denied by Muslim Bosnian Diplomats in London whom I met in March 2006.

Back to the pre-Dayton climate of 1995 September, the UN was in confusion, including the beleagured Secretary-General Boutros-Boutros Ghali, who was isolated and perhaps ignored by Bush (Snr) and the Clinton administration, who felt he was neither sufficiently diplomatic nor had the leadership qualities to deal with the needs and demands of the UNPROFOR Generals in the field. Generals like our own Michael Rose and later Rupert Smith, did not or could not work effectively with the 'weak' and 'moody' Secretary General. It is an irony, that when the opportunity arose for peace, people like Holbrooke – Bildt and Ivannov (Russian) were able to deal with the Bosnia stalemate better than UNs Boutros Ghali.

There was a "Hurting Stalemate"[1]. According to Susan Woodward, eminent peace/conflict resolutionist in Bosnia and Herzegovina by September/ October, there was a condition of not only deep fatigue, and shock and forlornness, but the three combatants were experiencing a classic bout of a hurting stalemate. She explains that the Serb-Bosnians were affected by Srebrenica and the defeats in the Krajina and also economic sanctions in Belgrade; The Croats had achieved enough hegemonic gains to contain the Serbs, and the Muslims were 'shattered' by the scale of the Sarajevo siege and the massacres at Srebrenica and Drina River Basin.

There was a 'stalemate' a sense of fatigue and hopelessness, that enough damage and blood letting had occurred in Bosnia and Herzegovina and the ethnic balance was being so disturbed both economically and psychologically.

In this "classic" syndrome of fatigue/ hurting stalemate, the three warring Presidents were ready and reluctantly willing to "kick" the ball of peace! In rode, US Richard Holbrooke and others with the full influence of NATO and the EU and American "knee-jerk diplomacy" to exploit and harness the hurting stalemate. Even the cruel, Demi-God like General Ratko Mladic is heard to have said – four years of blood-letting in the Balkans was enough, par for the four years of the two world wars that savaged the Balkans before in 1914-18 war and 1939-5 war period in former Yugoslavia.

Back to the Dayton Accords, let me briefly give you the basic features of the framework agreement signed in December 1995 in the Paris Peace Conference.

First the territorial integrity of Bosnia and Herzegovina was preserved with small adjustments to the pre-1991 boundaries externally. **Second** Bosnia and Herzegovina was divided into three sectors/entities as was the case in 1994. The Republika Sprksa of the semi-autonomous Serb-Bosnian entity with Banja Luka as the northern administrative capital.

Third The Federation of Muslim Bosnian and Croat Bosnians with over 42% of land territory of Bosnia and Herzegovina. And there was in the South Mostar – a divided city between the Muslims and Croat Bosnians, with the district of Broko in the north-east as a free land corridor between the three entities to be administered at district level.

Fourth There was to be a three tier presidency for Bosnia and Herzegovina with three elected ethnic political heads of state for the three entities. There was to be one national Prime Minister in Sarajevo for the whole state of Bosnia and Herzegovina.

Fifth The army, police, judiciary had entity level and national levels. Similarly the public sector had national, federal and ethnic (republic) levels of municipal and sector administrations.

Sixth To co-ordinate this fragile and multi-tiered peace framework NATO and non-NATO personnel vested with overall security responsibility. "IFOR" (Implementation force) of some 60,000 multi-lateral forces included a third from US ground troops including British, French, and even Russian were fielded by the framework agreement in December 1995.

Seventh An office of OHR (Office of High Representative) vested with authority from the framework powers, and the European Union, was given major administrative and overall responsibility to deliver the peace agreement. Lord Ashdown of UK served in the role with some distinction for 2003-2006 period and now we have a German Diplomat Herr Christain Shilling as the resident High Representative in Sarajevo.

Eigth The Dayton Framework Accords enabled the OHR to draw upon considerable help, advice and expertise from OSCE NATO/now EUFOR after SFOR, UNHCR, UNDP, ICMP, ICRC, and other IGOs and NGOs in Bosnia and Herzegovina.

Over the period 1995/6 to 2005 the ten years in Bosnia, Herzegovina has had major development assistance from the EU/UN/Council of Europe and other friendly agencies. Paddy Ashdown when he handed over his commission as High Representative to Herr Shilling said "A miracle since Dayton has happened in Bosnia". It is true a country devastated by a cruel and long ethnic war has recovered, when I was there in July 2006, I witnessed the work of all concerned, none more so than the brave people of Bosnia and Herzegovina. But all is not rosy in the garden.

Let me illustrate with my experience and meetings there, some of the Dayton shortcomings and failures to date. **First** Due to an over-whelmingly large IGO/NGO presence in Bosnia, the ordinary people young and old feel marginalized. Very high unemployment, poor training/skills, and lack of empowerment and lack of true democracy. **Second** The ethnic political elites of Bosnia are held to be ineffective and corrupt, in a dependency mode, on the OHR/OSCE/EUFOR etc. etc. **Third** Corruption is endemic at national entity and municipal level. Bribery and nepotism are rife even in employment and Amnesty International have found bias in the job markets . **Fourth** There is no real sense of Bosnian Nationhood, the Dayton agreement perpetrated old ethnic divisions. **Fifth** The sense of justice, respect for Human rights for people is very slow as the judicial processes are too bureaucratic and ethno-centric. **Sixth** Young people in Bosnia , are disillusioned, feel alientated and lost still in 2006 feel the Dayton process only stopped the war, but has not created a 'just and prosperous peace'. **Finally** The older people are languishing with only memories of Tito and the days of stability and social welfare provided. They are yearning for a new "Tito", electoral and political interest is low, amongst the young and even the old as they feel current ethnic political leaders are too parochial and selfish. Much is expected of new politicians in the coming general elections in October. This is a bewildering list of grievances of the Bosnian people, more so amongst the Muslims, who feel justice has not been meted for Serb/Croat excesses of 1991-5 including Srebrenica. Let me now give a brief run-down of the work of some efforts of the Principal Dayton framework organisations.

The OHR The Office of High Representative in Bosnia and Herzegovina. The mandate of the High Representative derives from the General Framework agreement of the Peace of 14th December 1995. (The Dayton Paris Peace Accords). The OHR is responsible for co-ordinating the implementation of the civilian aspects of the peace agreement.

The OHR has achieved success in repairing and re-structuring the civil Infra-structure of the country – housing, roads, bridges, and utilities and the return of over one million IDPs and refugees. Bosnia has a stable currency and normal diplomatic relations with its neighbours. The OHR works closely with EUFOR and with NATO. The OSCE is one of the principal institutions, along with UNHCR who have worked well in partnership to re-habilitate the people and to re-construct the war torn economy and infrastructure.

The OHR is 'double-hatted' as a European Union Special Representative (EUSR). The EU has "pumped" in a lot of Euros and technical assistance to sustain peace in Bosnia. Peace is now after eleven years self-sustaining, but the country still faces formidable challenges, to build effective civil society institutions to strengthen the rule of law, to reform dramatically the policing system, and transform its defence and intelligence force on non-ethnic lines, and to restore effective parliamentary democracy.

The OHR 'MIP' (Mission implentation plan) sets out its core tasks, remaining to be achieved. There is a Peace Implementation Council (PIC) and a steering board to assist the OHR. OHR cannot and should not do everything. Their mission is peace implentation, Bosnia is a country in transition, the job of the OHR, it is held is to over-see that Bosnia becomes a wholly modern economy capable and fit to join the EU.

Lord Ashdown says the OHR made significant progress in 2003-2004 with its achievements being:-

* Establishing a state level high judicial and prosecutional council
* Establish a Bosnia and Herzegovina wide Ministry of Defence
* Launching fundamental reform of Bosnia and Herzegovina system of indirect taxation and revenue collection.
* Unifying the city of Mostar
* Merging the entity intelligence agencies into one state level service.

For 2005 the OHR mission has been to focus on

1. Entrenching the rule of law
2. Reforming the economy
3. Strengthening the democratic capability of Bosnia and Herzegovina
4. Governing institutions especially at national and entity level
5. Embedding defence and intelligence sector reform so as to facilitate into Euro-Atlantic Structures for PFP (Partnership for Peace)

The OHR in Bosnia is however too obstrusive in my view, and all pervading still, it has a major co-ordinating role, but personally I believe it is now too patronising and rather too bureaucratic and should be wound up as soon as the Bosnia and Herzegovina structures and institutions are strong. Bosnia must not be "molly-cuddled" too much by the EU/EUFOR/OHR whereas UNHCR and OSCE have performed yeoman service to Bosnia.

Another area where the OHR is working towards is national banking supervision at non-entity level. Bosnia needs a de-regulated and liberalised banking network at national level, not as currently where there are indigenous and weak banks in Republika Sprska and other levels. In order to join the EU banking and credit institutions in Bosnia and Herzegovina need to be brought up to EU wide level.

The OHR, itself has not been helpful towards my research visit, sad to say of all the Dayton Framework Partners, the current office holder – has ignored two of the letters and several phone calls for help, in England and whilst I was in Sarajevo. Their Bosnian staff appear to be bureaucratic, aloof and security obsessed when I asked for routine information, even their press office reacted to me too late and too little, unlike OSCE, UNHCR, UNDP, EUFOR and other partners of Dayton, where I had a more welcoming reception and help for my book. Perhaps this is an occupational weakness of the OHR not only the current German one, but the previous one, our own Lord Ashdown was just as unhelpful to my need for help to write the book.

On a more positive note, Herr Christian-Shilling current OHR made his first visit to the Srebrenica Potoceri Memorial on 26th June, which I shared with him. Let me now focus on the 'goodies' of Dayton, where I appreciated help and advise in London and in Sarajevo during my visit.

Firstly, OSCE is vested with Dayton Framework agreement objectives to bring about a democratic society underpinned by the rule of law in Bosnia and Herzegovina.

The Dayton Accords, assigned the OSCE mission their responsibility for fair elections, human rights and regional military stabilisation, with the task of democracy-building added subsequently. These are OSCE's core objectives per their mission statement.

The longterm goal of the OSCE and International community is to support the establishment of institutions and processes that will ensure Bosnia and Herzegovina's survival as an independent state.

In OSCE's mission statement (website August 06) it states "such a state should have a political structure that produces dynamic and effective **governance** at all levels, and that guarantees the protection of human rights and the rule of law".

OSCE – from 1951, the Council of Europe, has considerable expertise for early warning, conflict prevention, crisis management and post-conflict rehabilitation in Europe, OSCE. I am pleased to say, is playing a lead role in Bosnia and Herzegovina. OSCE has a large HO and Field operation in Bosnia and Herzegovina, based at Sarajevo and four regional centres, Tuzla, Banja Luka, Mostar and Sarajevo, itself with 20 field offices covering the entire country.

Also it also has six political resource centres, which provide political parties, independent candidates and citizen groups with necessary resources to participate in the creation of a pluralistic and multi-ethnic political environment.

The missions work is divided into the categories of

- Education
- Democratisation
- Human Rights
- Security Co-operation

it has a wide spread field presence which enables it to work closely with local population/ politicians and officials. OSCE has an all-pervading and effective presence in Bosnia and Herzegovina through-out the whole country. I counted 47/ four wheel drive vehicles, and six CD limousines, parked just at their Sarajevo Headquarters office tower, an impressive presence, and I felt they are doing good work unlike the hidden presence of OHR.

The head of OSCE in Bosnia Ambassador Douglas Davidson is to me more in control and able to provide leadership with his presence and mission, this is based on my field research in Bosnia and Herzegovina. Ambassador Davidson is respected for his work on refugee returns, and plea bargaining agreement. Also to the right to Education and unified schools for all children, and underpinning Bosnia and Herzegovina, to adherence to International Human Rights law, treaties and conventions, many of which the country has ratified.

On the question of Human Rights, I am not yet sure whether OSCE can guarantee fundamental HR law, particularly in view of adverse reports I received from the ICMP, Srebrenica and Zepa Mothers Association and Amnesty International who all agree there is more work to be done to ensure Bosnia and Herzegovina is compliant to the UDHR, and other 'cannons' of International Human Rights standards.

One area of concern, both for Amnesty International and the people in Bosnia and Herzegovina, the employment base in certain parts the Republika and Federation entity level of treatment of ethnic bias in many job sectors, in particular in Croat areas for preference for their own ethnic applicants in job sectors like construction and other civil sectors. The OSCE and Bosnia and Herzegovina national officers need to accelerate programmes soon of job market re-regulation to embrace all applicants, regardless of ethnic background, in order to employ the most educated and skilled and not on ethnic lines.

Let me now move away from OSCE and focus on EUFOR (EU Force) another very vibrant and helpful organisation upholding the Dayton Accords. EUFOR is the successor to IFOR and SFOR 2/12/2004 which took over the responsibility in Bosnia and Herzegovina to provide a safe and secure environment there. In 2005 it assumed command of over 7000 troops from 22 EU member states and eleven non-EU troop contributing nations.

The force is divided into three military area operations, for the multi-national task force, first commended by major general David Leakey of Britain in 2004-5, and now under an Italian Major-General Gian Marco Chiavinc, who is stationed at Butmir HQ at Sarajevo airport. Major General Chivani is assisted by three sector commanders –

   North west – British

   North - Austrian

   South – Mixed commands

There are two divisions, the IPU (Integrated Police Unit) covering the whole of Bosnia and Herzegovina, and theatre troops spread out over the country.

Whilst I was in Sarajevo, I was able to maintain contact with Lt Commander Karen Halsey, Chief Media Spokeswoman of EUFOR, who was most helpful to my work.

In addition to compliance with Dayton Accord Chapter VII requirements, EUFOR are performing good and valuable help to the ICTFY, Prosecutors, to bring (PIFWC) – Persons indicted for War Crimes in Bosnia and Herzegovina, to Justice, also they are a back up to the Bosnia and Herzegovina Police units and work closely with EUMP (European Police) and close liason with NATO personnel.

EUFOR are engaged in mine/ ordinance clearance work with local personnel and NGOs provide technical and logistical assistance at public events, where a safe and secure environment is guaranteed.

EUFOR are also helping with arrest and search for illegal and illicit weapons practises of ethnic entities. It was only in early August 2006 that EUFOR had arrested some arms traders and illicit arms houses, whom they had taken into custody, in North-West Bosnia, arresting three Bosnian men, in possession of illegal arsenal of weapons, rocket launcher, land mines, grenades, pistols and 700 rounds of ammunition. (A.P./International Herald Tribune 4/8/06).

In January 2006, EUFOR was able to arrest war criminal Dragomir Abzazovic, where he was apprehended after the shootings in Rogatica. EUFOR troops fired in self defence. Three people in target house were injured. This was to help the prosecutor of the Canton Court in Bosnia and Herzegovina. However EUFOR nor its counter-part NATO, have been able to trace and apprehend the worst two war criminals at large Messers Radavan Karadzic and General Ratko Mladic. I have been informed unofficially that the net is fast closing in on these two ICPWs who are being harboured; not in Bosnia and Herzegovina, but in Slovenia and Serbia, according to unconfirmed reports.

In addition EUFOR is engaged in SAP (Stabilisation and Association Process) for Bosnia and Herzegovina, to apply for accession to the EU. This is co-operation with OSCE to establish integrated Army and Police structures in Bosnia and Herzegovina, at National level and not at entity level. At Sarajevo and even in outlying Republika Sprksa in my visit to Srebrenica/Potacari memorial I was comforted by the omnipresence of friendly EUFOR troops, cheerfully performing their duties of providing Bosnia and Herzegovina, a safe and secure environment. It was truly multi-lateral and re-assuring for me by their general presence wearing their own country battle kit and flying their flags, Finns, German, Norwegian, Italian, Greek and many more troop contributing countries. I was informed by the cheerful and helpful Lt Commander Karen Halsey that even they had redoubtable Gukhas under the British contingent a few months back. Knowing the Gukhas as I do, from my several trips to Kathmandu, I slept in peace in my bed in BentBa˘sa Emona Hotel.

Let me turn now to our own UN agencies which are performing great and valuable humanitarian service in Bosnia and Herzegovina, both before and after the Dayton Accords were signed in 1995.

The UNHCR was vested by both UNPROFOR and Dayton Accords with being the primary and major body to deal with refugee and internally displaced peoples in Bosnia and Herzegovina.

I have had excellent rapport and help both in London and in Sarajevo from UNHCR staff who have not only been kind but very helpful with my work there. Being a thoroughly UN/Human Rights activist I am personally and professionally proud of the assistance I received from Peter Kesler and Majde Praljac (Eternal affairs officer Sarajevo) to whom I am indebted in my project in Bosnia and Herzegovina.

According to a valuable file of information given to me by Majde, UNHCR have dealt with over 500,000 returnees from abroad and also 400,000 IDPs who UNHCR are attempting to re-settle in Bosnia and Herzegovina since Dayton.

Minority Returnees:-

    A. Federation of Bosnia and Herzegovina 272,597 to date

    B. Republika Sparksa   162,132

    C. Bracko District   21,382

In addition IDPs resettled in Federation about 91600 Republika Sparksa 87430 and Brako district 1997-8. It is significant from the data sheets, curtesy of Majde that the pattern of returns and IDPs settled, were very significant in 1996-2003 (7 year) period and since then, if the last three years have tapered down to some 60,000 of the total 571,820 returnees.

In deed there are massive numbers of people returning back 'home' after they ran away during the height of the fighting in 1991-5. UNHCR should be along with other UN agencies like UNDP, UNICEF and ILO commended for their sterling work. If only this is widely known by all through my book, the UN should feel proud to build peace in Bosnia and Herzegovina after its very poor record of peace-keeping and peace-making prior to Dayton. It shows that the UN specialised agencies like UNHCR, UNDP and others have a great role to play after war, or during war, when food and medical supplies were air lifted to Bosnia and Herzegovina, particularly to Sarajevans who are grateful for these humanitarian services, of which I am proud.

I was informed by Majde that UNHCR, mission has been so successful in its returnee/IDP re-settlement that they are down-sizing permanent presence in Bosnia and Herzegovina. It is truly a great job, done under very difficult conditions. The other agency of the UN family I am very proud to be associated with in my book and my visit to Bosnia and Herzegovina is the UNDP (see Appendices).

I have had long dealings with the UNDP in Cyprus, Belize, Sri Lanka, and Nepal, during my work for the UN, AI and VSO, in my younger days.

In Bosnia and Herzegovina during 1996 to 2006, ten year period UNDP has shown as equally as UNHCR as a premier UN agency helping peace-building in Bosnia and Herzegovina.

It has delivered over US $150 million in funds to support development of Bosnia and Herzegovina working towards a vision of a peaceful, prosperous, safe and stable Bosnia and Herzegovina, UNDP can boast of many tangible results:

1. Rebuilding Bosnia and Herzegovina's infrastructure with OSCE.
2. Bring home people with UNHCR
3. De-mining work in Bosnia and Herzegovina – over 900,000 sq. meters of prime land restored for socio-economic use mine clearance, capacity development with Bosnian Armed forces and EUFOR.

4. Destroying surplus guns in Bosnia and Herzegovina. To ensure security of citizens, over 100,000 small arms destroyed and 250 tons of ammo!!

5. **Reviving Srebrenica,** Boosting the Drina River basin economy in confidence building and ethnic co-operation after Srebrenica 1995.

6. Helping raise citizens voice in local government – education and enhancing civil society.

7. Shaping Public Administration help establish over 70% Bosnia and Herzegovina civil service since Dayton Training programmes for Civil Servants.

8. Developing an Information society on Bosnia and Herzegovina.

9. Providing Gender Equality – spearhead Gender law structures.

10. Help Bosnia and Herzegovina achieve MDGs uniquely tailored to national context and EU integration.

This is indeed a formidable list of goal posts – mapped out from 1996 Post Dayton todate, in which we can be proud of the UNDP's efforts, and UN system. After all war is nasty, but in peace and development we can be proud of the UNDPs work for the peoples of Bosnia and Herzegovina (see Appendices for UNDP Indices).

Two smaller units, NGOs or public bodies, I must refer to in my successful visit to Sarajevo for my research on Post Dayton re-construction, are the work of the British Council in Sarajevo and the lesser known Human Appeals International working in Sarajevo district, performing excellent service for the recovering people of Bosnia and Herzegovina.

The British Council has been working now for ten years in Sarajevo district. I was struck by their wonderful spirit and comraderie. Aisa their Information Manager is a "gem" and a fount of knowledge and help to me and all who go to the comfortable and friendly building in Ljbujanska, Sarajevo. It is a haven of peace, knowledge and books. The staff there are very helpful and long may the British Council work there to educate and inform the young of Bosnia and Herzegovina not only for education but peace-building and ethnic understanding for future harmony.

Last but not least the Human Appeals International, it was on the other side of the River from my hotel, in BentBaša's old cobbled streets. My curiosity was too much. One early morning after breakfast, I knocked at the friendly door of their office. I was greeted most civilly and friendly by two Arab persons from the UAE. Over Turkish coffee and iced water, I got to know the Finance Officer who was fellow Accountant Mohamed Yasir. I gathered they are a UAE HR Humanitarian organisation in Bosnia and Herzegovina principally in Sarajevo district helping deprived Muslim children who are re-habilitated after the traumas of the Sarajevo siege. Indeed I felt quite at home with HAI (UEA) in view of my own long children's rights and humanitarian work for developing countries.

Dayton is a "miracle" it has given Bosnia and Herzegovina an opportunity to recover from the cruel and sad war, but the people still need strong governance and empowerment and to gain enough confidence to join the EU in the future, as we shall see in the next chapter, Chapter 12.

1 Susan L. Woodward article p.p.139 'After the Peace' Eds.
2 UNDP report on SRRP (Srebrenice re-construction and rehabilitation)

Postcript 28th September 2006, on eve of General Election (1st October) in Bosnia (courtesy of Time Magazine 2/10/06 p.p. 36-38).
Andrew Purvis - writing from Banja Luke - the capital of the Serb-Bosnian Republika Sprska, asks can Bosnia's Peace Accords of Dayton Survive? He says "Pre-election (1st October 2006) posturing is bringing old ethnic and nationalist tensions to the surface throughout the region".

Milorad Dodik, the Prime Minister of Republika Sprska, a moderate is alleged to have said that his entity may try to secede from Bosnia and Herzegovina and ultimately join Serbia. Meanwhile Bosnian Muslim leaders in Sarajevo led by Haris Silazdzic, another moderate and a former Bosnian Muslim Prime Minister from 1994, told Time Magazine "The boundaries imposed by Dayton in November 1995, on ethnic lines should be erased because they are not natural - they are based on genocide".

Between these two moderates they have "cranked" up the heat for Bosnia's General Election. International officials and ordinary citizens fear a return to violence. "These two men are feeding off each other". They are not extremist ethnic nationals, but are using it to get elected. This is our current catastrophe says - Senod Pecanin, Editor of Sarajevo weekly Dani. He says - if current polls are correct they could wield significant political power.

On top of this political uncertainty the current OHR, is due to be scaled back, and some diluted authority in Bosnia is due to be handed over next year to a new EU Representative in Bosnia. The current OHR, Christian Schwarz Shilling told Time Magazine recently in Sarajevo – "There is a lot of fear, people remember the same rhetroic from the early 1990's".

Herr Shilling is of the view that return to war is unlikely, but Pecanin is less sanguine; for the first time since the war 1991-5, he said "I am afraid for peace here". The tensions are rooted in Dayton accords, as I have analysed in the book. We need to study not only the results of the General election (see Epilogue) but also assess the post election political and ethnic climate.

Silajdzic – wants a new dialogue, while his Serb-Bosnian rival Dodik says, they will fight attempts to dismantle the current ethnic entities. It is an anxious period for Bosnia, and mature political skills are needed for the country to sustain peace. Also the adverse repercussions in Bosnia could affect the Serbs and Albanians in neighbouring Kosovo and Belgrade.

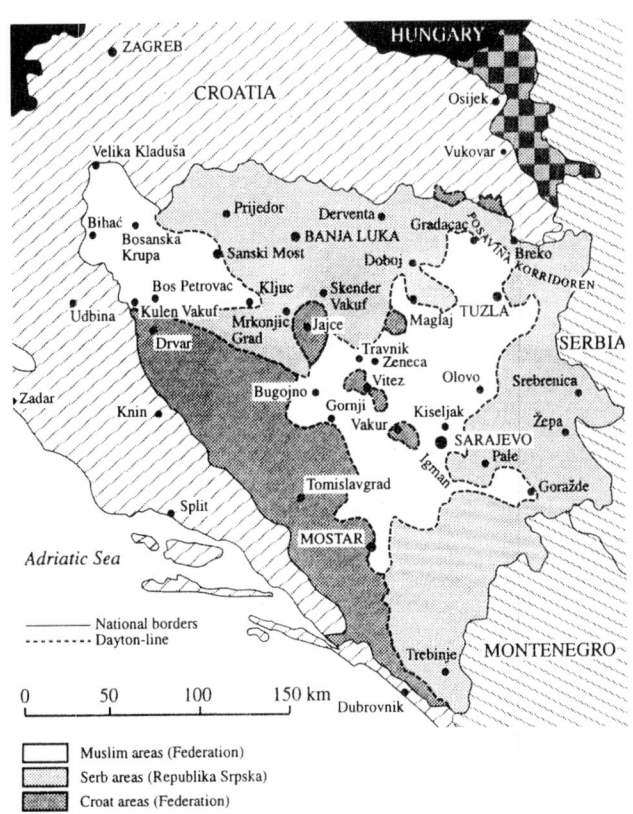

Bosnia-Herzegovina. The Dayton Agreement, December 1995.
(Courtesy of UNPROFOR).

Chapter Twelve

Bosnia and Herzegovina's prospects for Accession to the European Union

Before I embark on the pertinent question of Bosnia and Herzegovina readiness or compatibility to join the 27 EU members states, let me give my readers a brief country profile of Bosnia and Herzegovina.

Geography South-East Europe, bordering the Adriatic Sea and Croatia 44.00N, by 18.00E latitude/longitude

Land area 51,129 sq km, no sea area as such.

Total land 1,459km

>   Border countries – Croatia 932 sq km

>   Serbia – 527km. Coastline 20 sq km

Climate Hot summers and cold winters areas of high elevations. Severe winters, rainy.

Terrain – mountains and valleys. Mount Igman – well known. High point 2368m maglic.

Natural resources Coal, Iron ore, Bauxite, Copper, Lead, Zinc, Silver, Cobalt, Manganese, Dense forests and hydropower.

Land use arable land 19.6%

>   permanent crops 1.9%

>   others   78.5%

Environment Air pollution from metallurgic plants – considerable destruction of infra-structure due to 1992-5 war. Deafforestation.

Environmental International agreements. Party to air pollution. Biodiversity. Climate change. Law of sea. Ozone layer protection, wetlands signed but not ratified by state.

Politics Country is divided into joint Bosniac/ Croat federation (about 51%) and a Bosnian Serb-led Republika Sparksa or R.S. about 49%, the region of

Herzegovina in south is contiguous to Croatia and Serbia and Montenegro and this area traditional settled by Croat majority in the west, and an ethnic Serb majority in East.

Population about **4,458,976** (July 2006)

Age structure –	0-14 yr	15.5%	
	15-64yr	70.1% (male 52%, female 48%)	
	+65yrs	14.4%	
Median Age -	Total	38.4 yr	
	Male	37.2 yr	
	Female	39.5yr	

Population growth -	1.35% (2006)
Birth rate -	8.77 per 1000
Death rate -	8.27 per 1000
Net migration rate	13.05 per 1000
Infant mortality rate	total 9.82/1000 live births
Life expectancy	male 74.39 years
	female 81.88
HIV aids	less than 0.1% (2001)
Nationality	Bosnians, Herzegovinans
Bosniak (Muslim)	48%
Serb	37%
Croat	14.4%
Others	0.6%
Religions -	Muslim 40%, Orthodox Christian 31%,
	Roman Catholic 15%,
	Others 14% (including Jews)
Literacy rate -	age 15+ can read and write
	94.6% of population
	male 98.4%
	female 91.1% (2000 est)
Govt	Federal Democratic Republic
Capital -	Sarajevo city 800,000 people (as big as Manchester, UK)

National Day 23/11/1943 Tito's legacy)

Constitution – Based on the Dayton Agreement 14/12/1995

Executive branch -   Chairman of the Presidency
Sulejmen TIHIC (since 28/2/06)

Other members of three member presidency
rotating every eight months

Head of Govt (since Dec 02) – Chairman of
Council of Ministers – Adrian Terzic

Council of ministers – nominated by Council
Chairman (PM) approved by National House
of Representatives

Elections - the three members of Presidency, one Bosniak, one Serb and one Croat Bosnian, are elected by popular vote for a four year term on 5th October 2006.

Legislature Bicameral Parliamentary Assembly or **Skupstina** consists of national House of Representatives or Predstavnicki Dom. **42 seats** elected by proportional representation, 28 seats allocated from the Federation of Bitl, and 14 from Republika Sparksa;

Members are elected by popular vote to serve four year term

The Second Chamber is the House of Peoples – or Dom Naroda – 15 seats: five Bosniak, five Croat and five Serb members elected by the Bosniak/ Croat Federations, House of Reps and RS national assembly.

House of people serve four years at state/adm level. In addition at entity level: the Bosniak-Croat Federation – has a bicameral legislative – consisting of House of Reps (98 seats) and House of People (60 seats)

While RS has a National Assembly of 83 seats, and a 28 member Council of Peoples. Thus they have a large number of politicians at national and entity level.

Judicial Branch – Bosnia and Herzegovina Constitutional Court (9 members on ethnic lines) and three non-Bosnian members – appointed by European Court of Human Rights.

Bosnia or Herzegovina State Court (9 judges and three divisions – Administrative, Appellate and Criminal)

A Bosnia and Herzegovina War Crimes court opened in March 2005. Supreme Court cantonal courts in Federation and Municipal Courts in RS.

Flag description – a wide medium blue vertical band on the fly side with a yellow isosceles triangle abutting the band, and the top of the flag; the remainder of the flag is medium blue with seven full pointed white stars and two half star top and bottom along the hypotenuse of the triangle (v. complex, x impressive) (see illustration in appendix).

Economy Bosnia and Herzegovina is currently ranked next to Macedonia as the **poorest** republic of former Yugoslavia. Although agriculture is almost all in private hands, farms are small and inefficient and Bitt is a net importer of food. Industry remains greatly over-staffed, a "holdover" from the socialist planned economy of Tito. Military industries in Bosnia and Herzegovina established by Tito with not too much commercial potential and efficiency now. The inter-ethnic war of 1991-5 in Bosnia and Herzegovina, caused production to plummet by 80% from 1992 to 1995 and unemployment to soar. Output has recovered in 1996-99 and slowed in 2000-2, and some recovery again in 2003-5.

There is a thriving black market activity. The Konvertibilna mark (BAM) – national currency introduced in 1998, is "pegged" to the Euro and confidence in the currency and banking sector has increased recently. Privatisation has been slow, local entities only reluctantly support national level institutions.

Banking reform was accelerated in 2001, all Communist era payment bureaus were shut down, foreign banks formerly from West Europe now control most of the banking sector. There is sizable current account deficit and high unemployment rate remain.

The economy is bolstered by considerable EU and other reconstruction assistance and humanitarian aid from the International Community.

GDP $28.59 billion. There is a large informal sector in Bosnia and Herzegovina which controls over 50% of this GDP. GDP per capita -$6,800 (2005) about £3500 sectors-

agriculture   14.2%,

industry   30.8%
services   55%

Unemployment Rate - v. high 45.5% (2005) official rate; grey economy may reduce actual unemployment to 25% 30% (December 2004 estimate).

Population below poverty line – 25% (2004)

Inflation rate 1.4% (2005) stable ex consumer prices index.

National Budget   Revenue $4.373 Billion
                        Expenditure $4.401 B
Telephone system -   cellular 1.05 million (2003)
                        main line 928000

Telephone monopoly Bosnia Telecom need modernisation and expansion – no satellite earth stations competition and deregulation and opening of telecom market needed, to link to global standards. Internet users – 225,000 (in 2005)

Defence 4.5% of GDP on Defence/Military Expenditure too high for the weak economy.

Border disputes Bosnia and Herzegovina and Serbia have delinated most of their boundary but sections along Drina River valley remain in dispute. Discussions continue with Croatia on small disputes and maritime access.

Illicit drugs Minor transit point for marijuana and opiate trafficking routes to W. Europe. Bosnia and Herzegovina remain highly vulnerable to money laundering activity given cash-based and unregulated economy, weak law enforcement and instances of internal corruption and bribery very high.

Governance Weak at entity, national, and municipal levels. Need considerable work to comply with EU structures.[1] Having mapped out a comprehensive country profile – fact sheet at May 2006, let me now give you some of the principal criteria for Bosnia and Herzegovina, to accede to the EU. I shall use Hungary 1994-2004 as a case study when Hungary was engaged in full SAA talks to join the EU[2]

First Democracy and the rule of law.
Second Human Rights and Protection of minorities

Third Economic criteria

Fourth Liberalization of Economy

Fifth Economy in the perspective of membership of the EU

Sixth Internal market/ and free movement of capital, labour and goods.

Seventh Innovation.

Eigth Education, Skills, Training and Youth Policy.

Ninth Governance and civil society.

Ten Democracy/ Institutional change

Eleven Quality of life and environment

Twelve Justice and Home Affairs

Thirteen External policy – trade and international economic relations

Fourteen Common foreign and security policy

Fifteen Defence and Intelligence integrated structures.

These are 15 very important criteria and guidelines of the EU. "Acquis – Communitaire" (body corpus of EU rules) prior to Bosnia and Herzegovina joining the Union.

Further to my early research and observations in Bosnia and Herzegovina, I feel in a nutshell, the country needs to have a leap forward to comply with the 15 'bench marks' I have set out from the Hungary model, my belief and fear is Bosnia and Herzegovina is not ready yet, or for at least 8-10 years to obtain the necessary "Acquis" competences to join the Union. Perhaps another miracle like Dayton is needed for Bosnians to accede to the EU say by 2015 or so.

Another element currently in doubt of Bosnia and Herzegovina's early accession to the EU is the delicate subject of the PIWCs and the ICTFY in the Hague. There are still some indicted war criminals of ethnic origin both in Bosnia-Herzegovina and Serbia which will not only delay but definitely frustrate accession to the EU.

Croatia is fairly advanced in their negotiations towards accession to the EU. Croatia has already complied to many of the "15 Hungary" model sign posts, I have highlighted in this chapter. Also the arrest of Croat War Criminals and prosecution has had more success both in the Hague and in Croatian Courts. In the case of Bosnia and Herzegovina and Serbia, the arrest and justice to be meted out against the major PIWCs messrs Karadicz and Mladic and others will be a big obstacle to accession talks and eventual entry into the EU for both Bosnia and Herzegovina and Serbia.

In general Bosnia and Herzegovina, in addition to the war criminals issue have a great deal of work to do principally in market de-regulation, internal market liberalisation, banking and telecommunications and general economic sectors, reduction of gross unemployment, deficit reduction and budgetary adjustments.

In addition to above, governance and Human Rights compliance and the Rule of Law is weak in Bosnia and Herzegovina. Many years work needs to be done prior to compliance with EU Social Chapter 'Acquis' (rules). In the field of political institutions both at National and Entity level, both in Federation and RS levels, much work needs to be done to increase political, administrative and judicial processes to buttress weak civil society.

Bosnia and Herzegovina has only recovered from the brutal ethnic war after Dayton with enormous help from outside sources. It needs now to have a unified and universal attempt to forge new links not on narrow Ethno-Religious lines but on cross-border European links to take advantage of effective Democracy, Rule of Law, and Human Rights for all.

It is still a matter of concern that in the entities and at municipal level in RS and Federation and even in Mostar administration – pronounced ethnic-discrimination in employment, this is worrying for Human Rights activists including Human Right Watch and Amnesty International. Until and unless jobs are given and created to break down old ethnic competition and religious bias, Bosnia and Herzegovina's chances of joining the EU are slim and also levels of corruption in administration and within political elites will slow down the prospects of integrating into the EU job market and union status. There is a worry that due to major corruption and people and drug trafficking in Bulgaria and even Rumania's treatment of Roma minorities could frustrate their eventual full accession in January 2007.

I do not wish to under-estimate the task Bosnia and Herzegovina faces in order to join the EU, the country needs a new generation of leaders who are educated and skilled to think as Europeans and not be bogged down by narrow ethnic or sectarian mentality. Bosnia and Herzegovina has a vibrant young population and this generation I was privileged to meet and make friends with while I was in their country in July 2006. I felt they are crying out for change, for empowerment and wished to join Europe not purely for Economic reasons or trade, but for cultural re-emergence out of the ethnic morass they suffered from during1991-5 period and subsequently.

I feel bold enough to recommend to the young people they take their destiny in their hands, lose the narrow ethno-centric past and take to the globalized challenge of the 21st century by working towards the EU membership and the wider world. Be flexible, be prepared to change, be ready to travel and to integrate and not perpetuate ethno-hatred and religious separation.

I feel the Dayton constitution needs to be changed in order to deliver Bosnia and Herzegovina into modernity and to the EU. There is no place for a fragmented political structure of a sectarian federation and a Serb dominated Republika in the same country. Bosnia and Herzegovina needs nationhood of one country, one army, one police force, one banking system, and importantly a multi-cultural free state.

I believe and feel confident Bosnia and Herzegovina will join the EU but not yet. Perhaps by 2015, I may be too old to see that day as a 70 year old, but many of my younger friends in Sarajevo will be the "running" the country and will be proud EU citizens, like me, here in Britain.

I wish to conclude chapter 12 in a somewhat optimistic note, sharing with you the key economic indicators curtesy of the UNDP Early Warning System – Annual report of 2005.

"The Road to Europe"

Bosnia and Herzegovina's strategic goal is full and equal membership of the European Union. This is one of the long term goals about which there is a general consensus here. So UNDP asks how close is the country to attaining its goal.

There are key membership criteria that Bosnia and Herzegovina must meet. They include economic criteria set out in the Copenhagen and Maastricht Treaties. Essentially they relate to attaining adequate convergence with the level of development of core EU countries. "Without going into detailed analysis here we can compare Bosnia and Herzegovina with EU key economic indicators.

Bosnia and Herzegovina and EU (15 members/ 25 members) key economic criteria 2005

Indicators	EU (25)	Bosnia and Herzegovina
Real GDP growth %	2.4	5.7

GDP per capita (100)	87.9	7.3
Unemployment % of labour force	8.0	43.2
Inflation (CPI) annual average	2.1	0.4
Budget deficit % of GDP	2.6	0.1

Economic Indicator (cont)	(EU 25)	Bosnia and Herzegovina
Current Account deficit % on GDP	0.2%	17.3%
Public Debt as % GDP	63.8%	59.7%

On inflation, budget deficit and public debt (due to aid) is compatible with EU. On unemployment and current account deficit it is alarmingly high, and much work and adjustment is required. There are other key criteria, like the 'Hungary model' I have used, like Governance, Human Rights, Political Institutions, Banking/Trade de-regulation and other important social chapter compliance on which Bosnia and Herzegovina needs to set clear goals to succeed in the SAA talks and the road to Brussels; perhaps non more so than punishment of indicted war criminals and effective democratic governance (see appendices from United Nations Development Programme on Corruption and other early warning statistics 2005 report appended here.

Postscript 28th September 2006.
Courtesy of International Herald Tribune 27/9/06 "Anxiety as EU chief questions expansion".

"Aspirant countries fear a long wait"

Calls for a temporary halt to the expansion of the European Union, echoed by France and Germany sent "shivers" of anxiety through some of the countries seeking to join the EU. Said the President of EU Commission Manual Borroso, that the Institutional reform and the consititution for Europe will have to come before Bosnia, Serbia, Montenegro, Macedonia and Albania hope to join the Union.

This is even worrying Croatia who are advanced in their SAA negotiations. Having to wait till 2008 to progress SAA negotiations for the Balkans aspirants, including Bosnia and Herzegovina, could lead to de-stabilisation in the area, some experts such as Ivan Vejvoda, Executive Director fo the Balkan Trust, said "backtracking by Brussels could be detrimental for the West Balkans".

The Balkans trust warned that the region cold slide into ethnic nationalism and conflict if these countries were not offered a strong perspective by the EU consistent with a clear economic and political strategy.

I believe, the current vacilllations and delays in agreement on the derailed Euro-constitution could jeopardise chances of Bosnia and Herzegovina joining the EU in the next ten years, which in turn could exacerbate the ethnic and economic balance in the country and beyond.

References
1 Updated 16/5/2006. Source: The World Factbook – Bosnia and Herzegovina (2005/6)
www.gov/cia/publications/factbook/courtesy of Lord Corbett.House of Lords.UK
2 Source agenda 2000 Bulletin of European Union Commission u97 supplement.
3 International Hearld Tribune

Chapter Thirteen

Conclusion and Epilogue

I take my readers back to Chapter 1 of the book, it is a long journey from my great interest in ex-Yugoslavia from 1957, when Marshall Tito came to Kandy Sri Lanka to the present 2006, it is nearly 50 years, and it has taken patience, courage and determination to publish this book. My book is dedicated partly to better human rights and the rule of law in Bosnia and Herzegovina which suffered enormous cruelty and destruction in an ethnic-religious hegemonic war during 1991-95.

The darkest chapters of the Balkans wars, was Srebrenica where deliberate ethnic cleansing, mass rape and genocide resulted with the UN/NATO and the international community, unable or unwilling to prevent it.

It was only after July 1995, and the Serbs cruel and callous blood-letting in Srebrenica, that the US under the first Clinton-Gore administration decided to intervene with help from NATO and EU. The Dayton Accords stopped the ethnic wars, but its framework accords were built on ethnic and 'status quo' entities. Admittedly the Peace framework had to be tenable and acceptable to the three warring parties. Hence it did the job then in 1995 with courage and with the efforts of Richard Holbrooke, William Perry and Carl Bildt rather than Boutros-Ghali, and the beleagured UN peacekeepers. It is ironic and tragic that both the US and EU "ignored the weak Secretary-General, and perhaps unreasonably used him as a "fall guy", for the very failures and weaknesses of the UNSC, whose policies and decisions were questionable, particularly the early Arms Embargo, and its inability to give UNPROFOR a robust enough mandate with all the resources, men and material needed to make the 'Safe Areas' – Safe! It is an historic irony that the Safe areas of Srebrenica and Zepa were never 'safe', that even the arch-destroyer General Ratko-Mladic, said upon entering Srebrenica in triumph in July 1995, that the UN 'Dutch bat' of 370 troopers were too weak, and that he was the saviour of the Muslim population there, prior to the mass executions in the UN Safe Area.

As I pointed out in Chapter 8-9 even NATO with its massive air power, failed initially or was not clearly instructed by the UN diplomats – like Akashi and others to give help to the beleaguered UN forces and Muslim forces in July 1995. The red tape and misinformation in Srebrenica was great even the UN high command was bogged down by the poor communications between NATO and UN lines of control.

The Serbs knew this weakness and acted fast to misguide and "trick" the Dutch Bat in Srebrenica, even NATO command and control did not identify targets of Serb tanks and artillery pieces concealed in the forest. Also some UN Dutch bat personnel were taken hostages by the Serb forces, and also not given adequate support by Dutch politicians in Amsterdam.

It was tragic that the UN failed in the two safe areas, but was more robust and organised to defend Gorazde and Bihac enclaves with stronger Muslim support. Was there a conspiracy theory to sacrifice Srebrenica to the Serb forces by the Muslim High Command of President Aliza Izetbegovic in Northern Sarajevo to enable greater UN humanitarian assistance and to enable the Serbs to eventually lift the siege of Sarajevo.

I do not think there was a tacit agreement to sacrifice Srebrenica or to trade off Sarajevo to genocide in the enclave, but there are still some commentators 'peddling' that view and blaming UNPROFOR's in action.

The real problem for UNPROFOR was that it was not equipped with close air surveillance or air support from NATO to deal with Serb military strength. General Michael Rose and his men, managed to save Sarajevo, after terrible damage to both people and property there by "freeing" the Sarajevo airport (peace-making) and bringing in adequate supplies of food, medicine and other essentials to the people trapped there.

I believe UNPROFOR energy should have been devoted more to underwrite the Vance Owen Peace Proposals and later Stoltenberg-Owen package to the Muslims and Serbs, who in 1994 were not ready for peace. The UNSC failed and the US/EU failed in a twin-track "lift and strike" posture. I firmly am of the view that if the UNSC lifted the arms embargo and struck deep and hard with NATO bombing in July 1995, Srebrenica need not have happened. It is now no good trying to find excuses or reasons why it happened. It is evident that in 1992-3 the US/EU/contact group and UN were misjudged by the early Serbs determination to carve up Bosnia and Herzegovina with Croatia.

There was a loose agreement and strategy both by Slobaden Milosevic and Franco Tudjman to carve up Bosnia and Herzegovina amongst Greater Serbia and Croatia until the latter in 1994-5 set upon the Serbs in the Kin and Krajina and West Slavonia areas with crushing military gains, with German and US connivance.

The whole military and strategic balance changed in late 1994 and early 1995 in the Balkans. Even though the Arms embargo was now (1994-5) in 'tatters' the Economic sanctions on Belgrade and Serbia were being felt severely in the Serb capital, there was pressure on Milosevic to go to the Paris conference in Sept 1995 when NATO inflicted massive damage with major bombings. Messers Holbrooke, Carl Bildt (EU) and Vicktor Ivanov (Russian) were pressing the three exhausted and weary ethnic Presidents to agree to a formal ceasefire in Bosnia and Herzegovina.

The "hurting stalemate" concept of Susan Woodward was a realistic back cloth, to the situation in Bosnia and Herzegovina in October 1995, the three warring leaders felt they needed to safeguard what they had achieved, and agreed to stop the war, due to the stalemate, it was only the Muslim PM Haris Silajdzic and a few "belligerent leaders" who wanted further fighting to get more bargaining land in Bosnia and Herzegovina.

The Dayton accords to me stopped the war, but at a "terrible" prize, it has given Bosnia and Herzegovina, the best of two bad options: first dependence on NATO/EU structures, second a constitution with entities and a very complex political framework, which even now after eleven years of peace and re-construction is full of red-tape and inefficiency.

Reading Richard Holbrooke's epic of "How to End a War" I was both awestruck by his diligence and ability to deliver the Dayton accords to enable President Clinton to justify US involvment finally in November 1995, not only did they get us Congress approval for the Accord, but under-wrote it with nearly 15,000 – 20,000 US personnel to join a NATO led IFOR of 60,000 troops in Bosnia and Herzegovina by spring 1996.

Another fact of hot intense diplomacy which Holbrooke and Co, negotiated successfully with the Russian PM Chernmoydin in 1996 was to get them to agree to contributing to the multi-lateral force in Bosnia and Herzegovina. Just think after the end of the cold war in 1988-9, only seven years after both US and Russian troops were working for peace and reconstruction in South East Europe, a far cry from the Warsaw Pact – NATO hostile structures.

Another, not very known fact, I researched with Richard Holbrooke's help is the amazing story of gas supplies to Sarajevo in 1995-6. During the height of the Sarajevo siege, the Serb forces who encircled Sarajevo city, cut off gas and electricity and water to the Sarajevans, not only that, but the Serbs cipheoned off, valuable gas supplies away from the Muslims to their areas/sectors in Sarajevo, they did it by cleverly diverting the Gazprom pipeline from South Russia to the Balkans.

Whilst Holbrooke was busy with the ceasefire negotiations in Geneva in October 1995, other US officials like Steve Talbot and Leon Fuerth activated the VP Gore-PM-Chernomydin channel[1]. The Gore-Chernomydin dialogue enabled Bosnia and Herzegovina to secure gas, and later to get joint action by Russian and US personnel under IFOR. Holbrooke says "The issue for the Russians was not political but financial" the State monopoly of Gazprom were trying to "squeeze the logjam". Gas was not turned on until December 1995, when Dayton was signed in Paris.

War crimes indicted people like Mladic and Karadzic until they are arrested by NATO/EUFOR and punished in the Hague, thousands of the survivors in Srebrenica and Zepa, like the mothers, wives, and sisters of those two enclaves will not feel that the UN has helped in their enormous pain and "hatred" after eleven years as I felt for them when I visited them in their offices in Sarajevo. There are still fears for reaction of their arrests in Serbia and in Kosovo as an independent state.

It is a grim reminder to the UN and all human rights defenders that justice and respect for the law is not about signing UN conventions against genocide, ethnic cleansing and mass rape, but it is compliance with these standards that is important. In June 2006 there were interviews of some of the Dutch officials by women of Srebrenica and they came home somewhat happier to have shared the grief and pain with the UN Dutch officials who had reassured them of their own predicament in the dark days of Srebrenica where they were "let down" by NATO/UNSC and even by their Dutch political leaders in Amsterdam for not giving them the necessary power to stop the Serb forces. That is part of the continuing human tragedy of Srebrenica.

The mothers of Srebrenica are now wanting from their Government and the IGOs help to "bury the remains" of several thousand of their relatives not as yet still given proper Muslim burials in tune with their customs. So much for Holbrooke and his team of brilliant diplomats, which was backed by massive strong arm NATO air power; Dayton had to work for the sake of International sanity and US/EU power.

The question of a Serbdom dream of Milosevic, Karadzic and Mladic was shattered, and it is no longer viable, especially after the death of Milosevic in 2002, only partly prosecuted by her adversary Carla-del Ponte, chief prosecutor of the UN War Crimes Tribunal in the Hague, and the Kosovo embroglio.

I firmly believe here is another 'white elephant' of the UNSC, which has not yet fulfilled its role to mete out International Justice and standards which will heal wounds in Bosnia and Herzegovina, and also restore the credibility of the UN and International law.

Another area of concern I have for Bosnia and Herzegovina, and its survivors of the Srebrenica tragedy, they need to find both spiritual and economic compensation, for the loss of their loved ones. There is a deep sense of anger and frustration with their local political elites, and sometimes with the International Community, including British Peace-keepers and more so against the Dutch UN personnel.

They asked me, when I go back to Britain, to inform the people there, that they are still looking for justice and peace after the gruesome actions of the Serb-occupying forces who they said not only executed their husbands, sons and boys, but crully "quartered" the bodies and poured gas and chemicals to help desecrate the remains of the dead. I shall never forget the expression of those brave women and their continued courage in seeking their victims remains which is only human. They are also working hard in income generating schemes to supplement their project funds.

On the vexed question of Srebrenica type-genocide will it occur again, in the 21st century in another place, it is difficult to surpass the scale of the Serb cruelty. I saw the evidence in Potocari and Srebrenica, I would not wish to even hazard a guess, to assessing that it may recur, I hope and pray as a human being, that it should not happen again, but man's bigoted cruelty to their fellow beings are occurring in Darfur and other parts of the world even now, but the scale and sheer cruelty of Srebrenica will remain in my mind for ever.

Two more aspects of my book, need to be re-iterated, in this concluding chapter and that is how the UN is perceived there after eleven years, post Srebrenica and Dayton accords, and secondly and finally, to return to the question of prospects for Bosnia to join the European Union in the next decade.

As far as the UN is concerned, it suffered in Bosnia and Herzegovina, from early failures of UNPROFOR to keep the peace or to "protect" the people of Bosnia and Herzegovina. It is an irony that the UNSC named it a protection force, when it was only given a limited mandate and equally sparse resources in men and equipment.

It was first sent to the Croat border, to keep the peace in 1991-2 at the height of the Serb advances and fall of Vukavor and in East Croatia, where the UNPROFOR Command was weak and unable to separate the combatants or diffuse the conflict.

In 1993 to compound its early mistakes, the UNSC created the UN Safe Areas, not only for Srebrenica and Zepa but also for three more Muslim areas – this was both strategically and militarily ill-thought out. The Safe Areas concept was a French idea, which the UN adopted without proper logistics, military or humanitarian capability. It did not have full enforceability credence with close air support for which UNPROFOR was dependant on NATO.

The UN arms embargo again well meant to contain the Yugoslavia vortex did not work or was not adhered to even by the Germans, Italians and later the US. It was a diplomatic apology comparable to taking candy away from recalcitrant brats, who were intent on breaching the embargo from its early days. The US wished to lift it, but Britain and France and some other EU countries wanted it continued.

On the question of UN successes, the sterling work of UNHCR stood out in the way it dealt with food, medical supplies and other essentials, of course with help of UNPROFOR to the beleagured Sarajevans in 1992-4. UNPROFOR Generals like Lewis MacKenzie and Michael Rose did excellent work to keep Sarajevo airport open against Serb odds and later with their agreement to fly in aid and food.

Here I commend their bravery under difficult conditions. After Dayton again UNHCR and later UNDP have performed great service, both in receiving returnees and IDP's to re-settle them in Bosnia and Herzegovina. It is truly a great achievement by the UN specialised agencies like UNHCR, UNICEF, ILO and now UNDP who to me are re-deeming the presence and good name of the

United Nations in peace-building and infra-structure re-construction in Bosnia and Herzegovina.

Lastly but not least on the important question of Bosnia and Herzegovina's readiness and ability to join the EU, my considered view is NO, not yet, it may take on a conservative estimate over ten years more, Bosnia and Herzegovina to accede fully into the EU. Hungary (my model) and even Czech Republic, Slovakia and Poland took over ten years of preparation and compliance with the minimum "Acquis" requirements. Let us not forget we in the UK took nearly 20 years in our successful bid to join eventually in 1973 after a national referendum, and still in 2006 we have not joined the Euro.

Bosnia is on the right road, but Governance, Human Rights and Internal market requirements are still a long way from the Brussel's conditions to entry. On the question of Human Rights in Bosnia and Herzegovina, two things worry me. Firstly the employment legislation and the job market is still showing ethnic bias: Amnesty International in their recent reports "Bosnia and Herzegovina" – behind closed gates; ethnic discrimination in employment 16/06/2006 agree with me.

AI, considers that the process of returnees to Bosnia and Herzegovina is still affected by ethnic resettlement and job bias for homes and employment. Integration of returnees are not sustained free of discrimination, obstacles to sustainable return and durable integration of IDPs and returnees are still in 2006, a concern for the right to property and life which Bosnia and Herzegovina have enshrined in the Dayton accords – e.g. Alumniji Aluminium plant in Mostar and of the Ljubija Iron ore mines of North Prijedor R.S. are openly flouting workers rights and continue with ethnic discrimination.

Another area of grave concern on Human Rights compliance is the difficult problem of speedy prosecution of all PIWCs (Persons indicted for War Crimes) including the two classic cases of Karadicz and Mladic and some lesser PIWCs in the Hague and Bosnian Criminal Courts. It is essential both for UN/NATO to deal with this before the entry into EU is undermined for a long period.

I feel given the determination of the younger generation of Bosnia and Herzegovina, there is hope for that country, many women's organisations are working hard to engage in co-operative empowerment and small and medium sized enterprises of Sarajevo district and other hinterland areas are learning fast, that education, skills and employment are a key to Bosnia and Herzegovina's real future in Europe.

The preliminary talks of SAAs to accede to the EU started in November 2005, and whilst I was in Sarajevo in July 2006 it has captured the imagination of the citizens, the political elites have a major role to deliver their country to the EU.

Reference
1 Page 203 Shuttle for Peace "How to win a war" – Richard Holbrooke

Epilogue Since I concluded my research trip to Bosnia and completed my manuscript in September 2006, there were General Elections held in Bosnia on 1st October supervised by OSCE with 240 oberservers/monitors from Council of Europe (see Chapter 11, Postscript).

In my epilogue, I with to concentrate on some valuable late material received from UNDP (courtesy of Early Warning Report 2005/6, on following indicators (see appendix 1) –

1. The Ethnic Relations
2. Human Rights
3. Governance
4. Public and Personal security
5. Corruption and bribery reports
6. Confidence in Institutional Stability in Bosnia and Herzegovina.

I comment briefly on this valuable data.

1. On ethnic relations the climate is better now, between ethnic politicians after successful negotiations on police reform and army integration. There is some continuing anxiety in Republika Sprksa where some Serb-Bosnian groups are "clamouring" for a referendum for separation, like in Montenegro.

2. There have been reports that in late August/September that some ethnic groups have desecrated the grave of President Alija Izetbegovic, this action is being investigated by Federation Police and EUFOR.

3. There have been arrests in the Republika, on Arms and explosives dumps in houses. Again this is being investigated by EUFOR and Police there.

4. On the question of Human Rights indicators, there are some anxiety for returnees and re-settlement of IDPs. There is evidence according (see UNHCR Appendices) to Amnesty International of ethnic discrimination in jobs, both in Morstar and in Republika.

5. On Political and Institutional stablity, there are some improvements (per UNDP) more so in Federation than in Republika areas.

6. On corruption and bribery and red-tape at Adminstravtive levels, according to UNDP there is more work to be done, especialy on SAA, negotiations for EU admission for Bosnia and Herzegovina.

I have highlighted three areas where the UNDP are cautious of Bosnia and Herzegovina's UN MDGs objectives.

1. Povety reduction – very high priority for certain parts of Bosnia and Herzegovina.

2. Secure gender equality and empowerment of women in Bosnia and Herzegovina. This is urgent to achieve this goal before 2015.

3. Build on International Partnership for Sustainable Development.

Here too – Jens Toyberg – Fradzeu the Ex-Resident Representative of Bosnia and Herzegovina's UNDP mission, says some work needs to be undertaken in the next 9-10 years before 2015.

To conclude the UNDP findings, I am attaching some statistics from UNDP, where Better Education for all in Bosnia and Herzegovina at National Entity and Municipal level are paramount for Bosnia and Herzegovina to comply with EU acquis (see Appendices).

Also I focus on some extracts from Carla del Ponte's Cheif Prosecutor of the ICTFY, in the Hague, interview with Andrew Purvis (courtesy Time Magazine 15/8/06).

It is felt before November 2007 (expected date for end of tribunal) International Justice must be meted out in Srebrenica for Genocide perpetrated by Mladic and Karadicz, still at large in Serbia. Carla Ponte – says it is "paramount for justice" to be done to atone for Srebrenica.

Extracts of Carla del Ponte, Chief Prosecutor of ICTFY, interview with Andrew Purvis of Time Magazine (issue 21/08/06):

Purvis – "After 13 years the UN tribunal is nearing the end of its work. Has it been worthwhile?"

Del Ponte – "Definitely yes."

Purvis – "Why is the new trial – concerning the massacre at Srebrenica – important"?

Del Ponte – "It was a genocide, one of the greatest crimes you can imagine and it happened such a short time ago. Also after the death of Serbian President Slobodan Milosevic we have yet to hand out justice to the political and military criminals who planned, organised and executed this genocide."
Purvis – "You say General Mladic is still in Serbia, how do you know"?
Del Ponte – "I have my own information. I have my own tracking team and information from the Serbian government in Belgrade."
Purvis – "So is the Government in Belgrade hiding him, or are they just incompetent"?
Del Ponte – "Neither, I identified three times between end of 2005, and beginning of 2006, that Serbia could have arrested him and instead they sent him a message asking him to voluntarily surrender." (April 2006). "They don't want to arrest him because they feel it could be politically damaging".

This is a remarkably frank but a weak response from the Chief Prosecutor of the UN Tribunal. I believe having done my extensive research that both Del Ponte, the UNSC and NATO are culpable as the Serbian Government who are "harbouring" the War Criminals like General Mladic and Radovan Karadicz.

Del Ponte, must be replaced or asked to do her job, of prosecuting these two war criminals, or the Tribunal must be rapped up by the UNSC. The trouble and tragedy of this whole saga of a weak ICTFY is that UN/NATO fear that there will be de-stablisation fo the whole area. The "Kosovo Problem" may errupt in Serbia if these two War Criminals are punished. I think it is an affront to International Justice, and as the survivors of Srebrenica are still in pain and crying out for Justice and compensation.

Postscript 3/10/06. Bosnia and Herzegovina General Elections 1st October 06, early results courtesy of British Council – Sarajevo per e-mail 3rd October, 2006 and UNHCR.

1 Total electorate – 2,755,207 including postal voters. Total number of Candidates 7,245. Number of Political Parties 36, 8 coalition and 12 independent candidates.

Total turn out over 55% including many young/first time voters. Elections were incident free and according to EU/OSCE Monitors, fair. Elections organised and results were carried out by Centraina izboma komisija – Bosnia Herzegovina. Early results, The Tri-Partite Presidency of Bosina Herzegovina (per Dayton Accords).

Haris Silajadiz (Bosnia and Herzegovina-wide – (Ex SDA Prime Minister 1993-5) now PBIH. Zeljko Kosmic – SDP and Nebojsa Radmanvoic (SNSD).

Elections were held also for House of Representatives – Assembly of Bosnia Herzegovina, The House of Representatives of the Federation of Bosnia Herzegovina, The President and Vice-President of Republika Srpska-elected. Milan Jelic (SNSD) and the two Vice-Presidents are Adil Osmanovic and Ivan Kmdlji – both SNSD.

The party that won an absolute majority in Republika Srpska were the SNSD, with Milorad Dodik – Chair of Ministers (PM).

Elections were held same day in the Peoples Assembly of the RS, and also the Canton assemblies of the Federation of Bosnia Herzegovina.

Results on Assemblies and Cantons and Municipalities have not been announced yet. It is known that 13 of the 36 Political parties have sufficient quotas of votes to enter the Bosnia Herzegovina Parliament.

It is too early for me to make a rational evaluation of the new political climate, than to say that the elections are considered fair and passed off without any ethnic incidents. The new Prime Minister for Bosnia Herzegovina is not sworn in yet, and I believe Bosnia is entering a significant political landscape after these elections on post Dayton reforms and EU accession talks.

The latest international views – courtesy of AFP (Agency Francé Pressé) Wire 3/10/2006, 3.00 pm:

"Bosnian nationalists lose vote, but winners even more radical".

"Croat, Muslim and Serb nationalists all lost the election, but the even more radical (Separatist) Milorad Dodik – SNSD, and moderate Silazdzic – PBiH, who were clear victors – and whose rhetoric has cast a shadow over the ethnically divided Bosnia.

The OHR and EUFORs continued presence in Bosnia Herzegovinia may need to be extended, I feel, so that a better political/ethnical climate can emerge from the latest water-shed elections.

Chapter Fourteen

Bibliography

1.Books and Thesis

David Rhode "End game" – The Betrayal and Fall of Srebrenica (CSM Pullizter Prize Award)

Richard Holbrooke "How to win a war"

Anna Cataldi "Letters from Sarajevo Siege"

General Lewis MacKenzie "Peacekeeper Road to Sarajevo"

Lord David Owen "Balkans Odyssey"

General Sir Michael Rose "Fighting for Peace"

Rt Hon Lord Ashdown "Diaries, vol 1. and 2" 1992-6

Michael Barrat-Brown "Yugoslavia – from Tito to Milosevic"

Boutross-boutros Ghali "Peace and the UN memoirs"

Bernard Sims "Unfinest Hour – Britain and the destruction of Bosnia"

Milos Stankovic "The Trusted Mole"

Tim Clancy "Bradt Guide to Bosnia"

Robert L. Rotstein and Susan Woodward eds. "After the Peace, Resistance and Reconciliation – a Hurting Stalemate"

Henry I Sokslski "An ounce of prevention"

Tim Judah "Destruction of Yugoslavia – the Serbs History Myth"

Nora Beloff "Tito's Flawed Legacy"

Rusmir Mahmutchajic "Sarajevo Essays – politics, ideology and tradition"

Dr Nina Caspersen PhD thesis 2005 "Ethnic conflict and competition in Balkans"

Matts Berdel "Bosnia and the Balkans crisis"

Wolfgang Bermen and Martin Vadest "UN Peacekeeping in Trouble – lessons from former Yugoslavia"

Carl Bildt "Peace keeping Journey"

Rt. Hon John Major "Autobiography – Harpers 1999"

Marrack Goulding "Peacemonger in Yugoslavia"

David Malone eds "Human Rights Violations – Threats to Peace and Security"

Danesh Sarooshi "The UN and Development of Collective Security" 1998

Eds Mary Kaldor "The Political economy of the war in Bosnia and

Herzegovina"

Madelene Albright "New/Order/Disorder memoirs in UN"

J.G. Ruggie "Winning the Peace" UNPROFOR 1996

2. Periodicals/Journals

UNDP - Early Warning System – country report Bosnia 2005/6

UNDP Bosnia and NDG Goals 2005

UNHCR Refugees Return 2005

OSCE Reports on Bosnia and Herzegovina ex Website 2006

OHR Website Reports 2006

EUFOR Website Reports 2006

Aktivnoski 2003/4 - Journal of the Mothers and Wives of Srebrenica and Zepa Enclaves victims

UN Secretary General's Report on Srebrenica A/54/549 – 1999

3. Leading Articles

Lord David Hannay "UN Safe Areas"

Dr Nina Caspersen "Fences round ethnicity"

Craig Smith (IHT New York) Bosnian Pride and Visoko Pyramids 16/5/06

Tom Walker and Jon Swan (Sarajevo) Sunday Times – Mladic $3 million offer for surrender fails 26/2/2006

Two Bosnian Newspapers 21/7/06 – Oslo bodenge and Dnevini Avaz.

4. UK Parliamentary Papers

Foreign Affairs Select Committee, report on West Balkans 2004-5 (courtesy of Lord Anderson of Swansea)

House of Lords – Hansard Report, 15th November, 2005 (courtesy of Lord Corbett of Casle Vale)

List of Acronyms and Abbreviations

Accords	Ohio USA Nov 2005
AI	Amnesty International
B and H	Bosnia and Herzegovina
CAS	Close Air Support (NATO)
Contact group	'US Britain France, Russia and Germany'
Cleansing	cleansing by Serbs, Croats, and Muslim to create homogenous ethnic areas.
Crime of Ethnic	This was a gross violation of human rights of ethnically
Crime of Genocide	Deliberate and Systematic action by one majority ethnic group to kill or eliminate another minority ethnic group in Srebrenica
CSM	Christian Science Monitor
Dayton Framework	Peace Treaty signed in Dec 1995 in Paris negotiated in Dayton
DPP	Tito's Secret Police Department of Protection of People
EC	The Commission of European Union in Brussels
ECHR	The European Court of Human Rights of the Convention of the European Human Rights
ECJ	European Union Court of Justice
EP	European Parliaments in Brussels and Strasborg
EU	European Union – 25 – 27 member states (Jan 2007)
EU compliance system.	In order to join the EU, new member states like Bosnia have to comply with the 'Acquis' of Maastricht and Copenhagen rules, see SAA
EUFOR	European Union Force (Multi-Lateral Force) 2004-6
EUMP	European Union Mission Police
EURO	The European Currency Zone of 15 EU member states from 2002 Acquis Communitaire This is a corpus of EU rules and procedures the member states have ratified in the EU Treaties of Rome, Nice, Maastricht and Amsterdam and others codified as EC law.
FAS	Full-scale Air Strikes
FYR	Former Yugoslavian Republics
HDZ	Croat Democratic Union
ICC	International Criminal Court
ICMP	International Commission for Missing Persons
IDP	Internally Displaced Persons

IFOR	Implementation Force Bosnia and Herzegovina 1995
ILO	International Labour Organisation
IWCTFY	International War Crimes Tribunal for Former Yugoslavia
"Lift and Strike policy"	The twin track strategy of the US to lift the UN arms embargo and strike/bomb with NATO
NATO	North Atlantic Treaty Organisation
OHR	Office of High Representative Post Dayton 1995-2006
OSCE	Organisation of Security and Co-operation in Europe (Council of Europe 1953-2006)
PBiH	Party of Bosnia and Herzegovonia
PFP	Partnership for Peace pre-NATO association.
Rape as an Act of War	This is now a war crime against humanity of rape of women, under war conditions on the ICC Statue of Rome
SAA	Stability and Accession agreements/negotiating to join EU as new Members
SDA	Social Democratic Alliance – Bosnian Muslims
SFOR	Stabilisation Force 2003-2004
SNSD	Serb-Party of Independent Social Democrats
SOP	Stoltenberg Owen Peace plan
SPD	Social Democratic Party
SRRP	UNDP's Srebrenica Reconstruction and Rehabilitation Programme
UN Convention against torture and Cruel, Inhuman, and degrading treatment	
UNESCO	United Nations Educational Scientific and Cultural org
UNDP	United Nations Development Programme
UNGA	United Nations General Assembly
UNHCR	United Nations High Commission for Refugees
UNICEF	United Nations Childrens Fund
UN-MDG	United Nations Millenium Development Goals from 2001-15 for Bosnia and Herzegovina (see UNDP report epilogue)
UN-P5	5 Permanent Great Powers of UN Security Council
UNPROFOR	United Nations Protection force 1991-5
UNSC	United Nations Security Council
UN Torture Convention and CID	
VOPP	Vance Owen Peace plan
VSO	Voluntary Services Overseas (UK Charity)
WHO	World Health Organisation

Appendices
Courtesy of UNDP

 ETHNIC RELATIONS

The Inter-ethnic Stability Index

The past year brought no major improvement in ethnic relations. In fact, a series of mostly political events during the year threatened ethnic stability.

During the first half of the year, these included failure to meet the EU Feasibility Study conditions, inability to agree on police reform, and crisis in the Council of Ministers.[1] An initiative by a grouping of RS civil society organizations also raised tensions, as it launched the issue of a referendum over secession by the RS from BiH. The RS Army oathtaking ceremony, or rather the refusal to take the oath, also had an impact.

During the second half of the year, the tenth anniversary of the Srebrenica massacre was commemorated, with politicians from both entities once again expressing very different attitudes and exacerbating ethnic tensions. The tenth anniversary of the Dayton Agreement was also marked, providing an additional opportunity for division, as the agreement continues to be subject to very different interpretations by the political leaders of the different ethnic groups.

There was progress in the final quarter of the year, as talks began between the leaders of the main political parties over constitutional change and a compromise was found for police reform. In fact, that compromise was the occasion for the most positive political and social event of the year, as the European Commission decided to let BiH begin negotiations on a Stability and Association Agreement. This had a positive impact on the Inter-ethnic Stability Index.

The Inter-ethnic Stability Index for Bosnia and Herzegovina

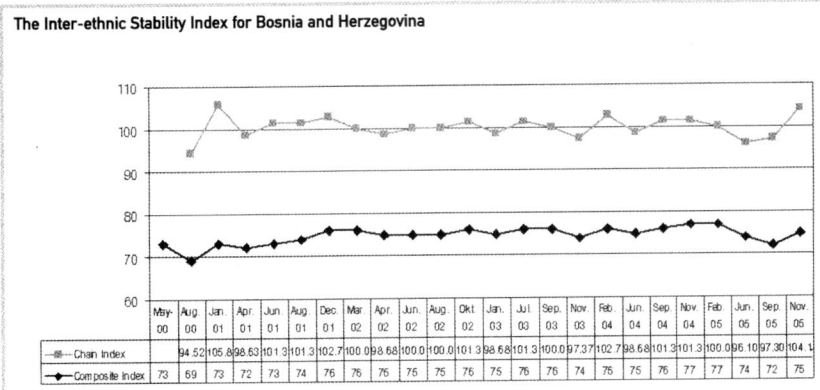

	May-00	Aug.00	Jan.01	Apr.01	Jun.01	Aug.01	Dec.01	Mar.02	Apr.02	Jun.02	Aug.02	Okt.02	Jan.03	Jul.03	Sep.03	Nov.03	Feb.04	Jun.04	Sep.04	Nov.04	Feb.05	Jun.05	Sep.05	Nov.05
Chain Index		94.52	105.8	98.53	101.3	101.3	102.7	100.0	98.68	100.0	100.0	101.3	98.68	101.3	100.0	97.37	102.7	98.68	101.3	101.3	100.0	96.10	97.30	104.1
Composite Index	73	69	73	72	73	74	76	76	76	76	75	76	75	76	76	74	76	75	76	77	77	74	72	75

1. Ethnicity and human rights violations

In this section we analyse two aspects of discrimination. The first is to what degree the public in the three majority areas thinks ethnic or religious discrimination exists where they live. We look at the views of both the majority and the minority populations. The second is the degree to which members of the minority populations think they have suffered actual discrimination.

---

38 1   See Section I for more details.

125

Table I

Think minority population civil or ethnic rights are discriminated against in their municipality of residence

	Total		Bosniak majority areas		Croat majority areas		Serb majority areas	
Survey	04/#4	05/#4	04/#4	05/#4	04/#4	05#4	04/#4	05#4
In %	9.1	5.38	8	3.07	9.9	5.09	10.3	8.39
Index 05/#4 - 04/#4	59.12		38.38		51.41		81.46	

Source: Opinion poll carried out for EWS by PRISM Research

Regarding the first question, we found that people were considerably less inclined to think discrimination existed in their community in the final quarter of 2005 than they had been in 2004, down from 9.1% to 5.38%. The level spiked during the year, however (esp. the second and third quarters), reflecting heightened tensions due to the long stand-off over police reform and EU negotiations. Resolution of the political problems relaxed these tensions and so also awareness of the potential for discrimation.

In Bosniak majority areas, awareness of discrimination has halved since the end of 2004 (from 8% to 3%). It had remained stable at last year's level for most of the year, only dropping in the final quarter of 2005. This was because trends affecting the majority and minority groups were contrary. While Bosniak acknowledgement of discrimination declined steadily over the year, minority population concerns rose to peak in the third quarter at 26%, only to fall in the final quarter to 11%. (Table I and II).

In Croat majority areas, the overall level rose from 9% at the end of 2004 to 16.8% during the second quarter of 2005. It dipped in the third but fell significantly only at the end of 2005, to 5% . This was the trend for both the majority and the minority population. Overall, the minority sample in these areas felt considerably less vulnerable at the end of 2005 than it had at the end of 2004 (down from 22.4% to 15.1%). (Table I and Table II).

In Serb majority areas, things deteriorated considerably during the second and third quarters, but improved in the final quarter of 2005, returning to levels very close to those at the end of 2004. As there was little or no change in the views of the majority population (stable around 10%), this improvement was entirely due to changes in minority opinion, which travelled from 26.9% at the end of 2004, through a peak of 36% in the third quarter, to fall to 13.4% in late 2005. (Tables I and II).

Although the situation deteriorated considerably during the middle of the year in response to political issues, it is worth stressing that the minority populations in all three areas are now much less likely to think discrimination exists in their community than they were a year ago: down by a third in Croat majority areas, from 22.4% to 15.1%, and by half in Serb majority areas, from 29.6% to 13.4%, to within a few percentage points of the level in Bosniak majority areas, now 11.6%. Majority opinion has changed far less, by comparison.

The pattern is very similar regarding the second issue. In Tables III and IV, we note that relatively small percentages of the minority samples in both Bosniak and Serb majority areas thought they had suffered ethnic discrimination both in late 2004 and late 2005 - around 4%. During the Summer, however, levels were considerably higher, peaking in the third quarter at 16.6% in Bosniak majority areas and 9.5% in Serb majority areas. Croat areas, in constrast, saw the level of discrimination reported by members of the minority sample decline steadily through the year, to approximately 6%.

Table II

Think minority population civil or ethnic rights are discriminated against in their municipality of residence

Area	Bosniak majority areas				Croat majority areas				Serb majority areas			
Sample	Maj. population		Min. population.		Maj. population		Min. population.		Maj. population		Min. population.	
Survey	04/#4	05/#4	04/#4	05/#4	04/#4	05/#4	04/#4	05/#4	04/#4	05/#4	04/#4	05#4
In%	6.4	3.1	15.4	11.6	7.3	5.1	22.4	15.1	6.2	8.4	29.6	13.4
Index 05/#4 - 04/#4	48.4		75.3		69.9		67.4		135.5		45.3	

Source: Opinion poll carried out for EWS by PRISM Research

Table III
'ave personally been discriminated against or felt deprived of their rights in their municipality of residence during the
ıst year because of their ethnicity

ea	Bosniak majority areas		Croat majority areas		Serb majority areas	
ınple	Minority population.		Minority population.		Minority population.	
ᵗ vey	04/#4	05/#4	04/#4	05/#4	04/#4	05#4
ᵗ	5.2	3.9	23.4	5.8	3.7	3.7
Index 05/#4 - 04/#4	75.00		24.79		100.00	

Source: Opinion poll carried out for EWS by PRISM Research

Psychological and sociological theories of ethnicity link intense sense of vulnerability or discrimination with higher levels of identification with the ethnic group. This is where one may find the reason for the predominance of ethnic affiliation over civic identity. To what degree the sense of vulnerability or discrimination may be considered objective and to what degree a defence mechanism or means to attain a concrete advantage is another question.

The pattern is similar with regard to discrimination on religious grounds, with the one exception that the minority sample in Bosniak majority areas was a little more likely to complain of religious than ethnic discrimination during the third quarter, while in the other majority areas the levels were the same. (Table IV in annex).

Overall, the trends suggest that both the belief that discrimation exists and the belief than one has been discriminated against personally are very sensitive to political tensions.

2. The return of refugees and displaced persons

The final quarterly report for 2005 included analysis of refugee return, based on data from UNHCR reports up to 31 October, 2005. The total number of returns was 5,885 (1,138 from abroad, 4,747 displaced persons from within BiH). The process of refugee return is clearly drawing to a close. The last ten years have seen more than 453,000 minority returns. Fewer than 6,000 took place this year. Of course, these figures do not show how many returnees actually tried to live in their pre-war homes after recovering their property, which is very important for any understanding of ethnic relations or the status of minority returnees. We will not have more precise data until a census is taken.(Table V and VI).

Acceptance of minority return is highest in Bosniak majority areas, though it has fallen slightly since the last quarter of the previous year (from 93.7% to 92.2%). Acceptance levels have fallen in Croat majority areas over the year (from 88.6% to 78.9%). The level in Serb majority areas at the end of 2004 was 77.5% but rose to 89.1% in the final quarter of 2005. (Table VIII).

Table VIII
Entirely or basically agree that people not of the local majority ethnicity who lived in this municipality before the war should return to their homes:

Area	Bosniak majority areas		Croat majority areas		Serb majority areas	
Survey	04/#4	05/#4	04/#4	05/#4	04/#4	05#4
In%	93.7	92.2	88.6	78.9	77.5	89.1
Index 05/#4 - 04/#4	98.40		89.05		114.97	

Source: Opinion poll carried out for EWS by PRISM Research

A crucial precondition for sustainable minority return and ethnic reconciliation is confronting the issue of war crimes. We monitor this through the public's acceptance of the thesis that reconciliation in BiH requires that all three ethnic groups be released from the burden of collective guilt by ensuring that war crimes suspects face trial. Our surveys showed significant oscillation in the different areas on this issue. (Table XI).

ANNEX

I   Political stability in BiH - Tables

Table I
As regards politics, things in BiH are getting?

Sample	All				Gender							
					Men				Women			
	Feb 05.	Jun 05.	Sep 05.	Nov 05.	Feb 05.	Jun 05.	Sep 05.	Nov 05.	Feb 05.	Jun 05.	Sep 05.	Nov 05.
	%	%	%	%	%	%	%	%	%	%	%	%
Worse	53.4	64.8	73.4	66.9	52.0	65.1	75.4	66.9	54.7	64.4	71.5	67.0
Better	34.3	22.1	18.8	22.9	34.6	21.8	18.5	23.0	34.1	22.4	19.2	22.7
DK/NA	12.3	13.1	7.8	10.2	13.4	13.1	6.2	10.0	11.2	13.2	9.3	10.3
Total	100.0	100.0	100.0	100.0	100.0	100.0	100.0	100.0	100.0	100.0	100.0	100.0

Table II
As regards politics, things in BiH are getting?

Sample	Bosniak majority areas				Croat majority areas				Serb majority areas			
	Feb 05.	Jun 05.	Sep 05.	Nov 05.	Feb 05.	Jun 05.	Sep 05.	Nov 05.	Feb 05.	Jun 05.	Sep 05.	Nov 05.
	%	%	%	%	%	%	%	%	%	%	%	%
Worse	52.1	65.7	71.4	74.9	39.6	54.6	58.0	54.6	60.9	68.3	82.3	62.4
Better	36.0	21.4	23.4	17.4	32.6	23.0	18.6	29.0	30.8	21.2	12.0	26.8
DK/NA	11.9	12.9	5.2	7.7	27.8	22.4	23.4	16.4	8.3	10.5	5.6	10.9
Total	100.0	100.0	100.0	100.0	100.0	100.0	100.0	100.0	100.0	100.0	100.0	100.0

Table III
Please rank the following issues in order of importance to you personally

Sample	All				Men				Women			
	Feb 05.	Jun 05.	Sep 05.	Nov 05.	Feb 05.	Jun 05.	Sep 05.	Nov 05.	Feb 05.	Jun 05.	Sep 05.	Nov 05.
Corruption	3.2	3.1	2.8	3.1	3.1	2.9	2.8	3.0	3.3	3.2	2.9	3.1
The economy (unemployment, low and irregular income, etc.)	2.0	1.9	2.0	2.0	1.9	1.9	2.1	2.0	2.0	1.9	1.9	2.0
The political situation	4.4	3.9	4.0	4.0	4.2	3.7	3.9	3.9	4.5	4.0	4.1	4.2
Crime	3.9	3.5	3.6	3.7	3.9	3.4	3.5	3.6	3.9	3.5	3.6	3.8
Youth emigration	4.6	5.0	4.8	4.7	4.6	5.1	4.8	4.7	4.6	4.8	4.8	4.7
Education	5.1	5.4	5.3	5.2	5.2	5.5	5.3	5.3	4.9	5.3	5.4	5.1
Health	4.8	5.3	5.3	4.9	4.9	5.4	5.3	4.9	4.6	5.2	5.2	4.9
The survival of BiH as a country	.	.	.	.	.	.	.	.	.	.	.	.
The survival of the FBiH	.	.	.	.	.	.	.	.	.	.	.	.
The survival of the RS	.	.	.	.	.	.	.	.	.	.	.	.

46

128

quarter of 2005, compared to 6.3% in Bosniak majority areas and 4.8% in the RS. Through the year, reported abuse of police powers was more common in urban than rural areas. (Table XIII).

On the other hand, fewer people reported having been arrested without warrant (personally or a family member) than in 2004. The percentage is less than 1% in all three majority areas, which it was not a year ago. During the second quarter, the picture deteriorted, but improved again over the following two quarters. (Table XVI).

Our surveys reveal a major fall in the police's approval rating compared to the final quarter of 2004 in Bosniak majority areas (from 60.3% to 50.9%), and an even greater one in Croat majority areas (from 71.7% to 48.6%). In the RS, the police approval rating in the final quarter of 2005 was higher than in late 2004 (66.3% up from 60.4%). We see similar trends regarding the courts and their approval rating, which has fallen in Bosniak and Croat majority areas, but risen in Serb ones. (Table XVII). ⬛⬛⬛

ANNUAL REPORT 2005
A YEAR IN REVIEW

PUBLIC AND PERSONAL SECURITY

The Safety Stability Index

The issue of security has been becoming less politicised. The problems no longer closely mirror political changes, being mostly tied to the socio-economic malaise affecting the country. The year saw a series of tragic individual stories and the high crime level is clear from press coverage. In contrast to the immediate post war period, when local minorities, particularly returnees, were the targets of violence and crime, it seems that only a small proportion of crime is now linked to ethnicity.

The key to tackling these problems in the long term is police reform, which the European Commission made a condition for entering upon any new phase in European integration.

Police reform became extremely politicized and has contributed to deepening ethnic divisions in the country. At the end of the year and under pressure for the international community, a compromise was reached which laid out the structure in principle and ensured that State-level security policy capacity will be strengthened. Nevertheless, the details have not been determined and are expected to be the topic of future political debate.

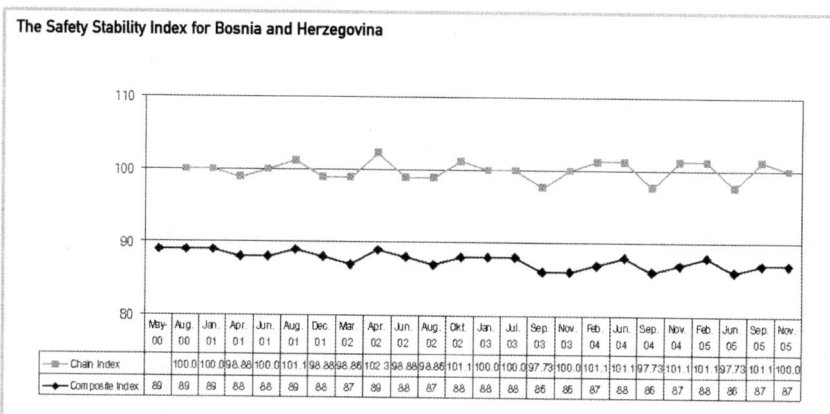

The Safety Stability Index for Bosnia and Herzegovina

	May-00	Aug. 00	Jan. 01	Apr. 01	Jun. 01	Aug. 01	Dec. 01	Mar. 02	Apr. 02	Jun. 02	Aug. 02	Okt. 02	Jan. 03	Jul. 03	Sep. 03	Nov. 03	Feb. 04	Jun. 04	Sep. 04	Nov. 04	Feb. 05	Jun. 05	Sep. 05	Nov. 05
Chain Index	100.0	100.0	98.88	100.0	101.1	98.88	98.86	102.3	98.88	98.86	101.1	100.0	100.0	97.73	100.0	101.1	101.1	97.73	101.1	101.1	97.73	101.1	100.0
Composite Index	89	89	89	88	88	89	88	87	89	88	87	88	88	88	86	86	87	88	86	87	88	86	87	87

1. Analysis of the main characteristics

There were no major developments in public safety last year in BiH, though there has been some fluctuation in crime levels.

Table I
Victims of during previous three months (personally or member of family):

	Total		Bosniak majority areas		Croat majority areas		Serb majority areas	
Survey	04/#4	05/#4	04/#4	05/#4	04/#4	05#4	04/#4	05#4
Burglary	1.4	1.2	2.8	1.4	0.5	1	0.2	1.2
Pick pocketing	1.1	1.9	1.1	1.4	0.5	4.7	1.4	1.7
Car theft	0.8	1.3	1.4	1	0.9	5.2	0	0.3

43

ANNUAL REPORT 2005
A YEAR IN REVIEW

Table VI
Has sought police assistance in previous three months (personally or a member of family)

	Total		Bosniak majority areas		Croat majority areas		Serb majority areas	
Survey	04/#4	05/#4	04/#4	05/#4	04/#4	05#4	04/#4	05#4
In%	4.9	6	7.9	5.7	6.8	15.7	1	3.4
Index 05/#4 - 04/#4	122.45		72.15		230.88		340.00	

Source: Opinion poll carried out for EWS by PRISM Research

Crime levels at the end of the year were not significantly different from what they had been a year previously. Our surveys show a rise in burglary, pickpocketing, and car theft, but the level is still below two percent and so within the margin of error. (Table I)

There appears to be some improvement in public safety in Bosniak majority areas. At the end of 2004, approximately 5.3% of the sample reported having suffered one of the forms of crime we monitor. That was down to 3.8% in late 2005. Results in the second quarter were more worrying, when 3.4% of the sample reported a break-in and 4.2% reported having been pick-pocketed. (Table I)

Crime levels are highest in Croat majority areas. The level is up significantly on the last quarter of 2004. In just a year, the percentage reporting having suffered a crimes has risen from 1.9% to 10.9%. Crime levels were rising through the year. This is an important trend and requires monitoring. (Table I)

Aggregate crime levels in the RS have doubled over the year, but from a low base: 1.6% to 3.2%. The results were a bit worse in the second quarter, but soon returned to their earlier level. (Table I)

In similar fashion, the public demand for police assistance has not changed much. Over the year, it rose from 4.9% to 6%. In the final quarter of 2005, as one might expect, demand was highest in Croat majority areas (15.7%), considerably lower in Bosniak majority areas (5.7%) and the RS (3.4%). (Table VI)

Levels of satisfaction with police assistance varied considerably over the year, with discrepant trends in the three majority areas. In Bosniak majority areas, satisfaction levels rose from 21.8% at the end of 2004 to as high as 41.4% by the end of 2005. (Table IX)

The trend in Croat majority areas was directly opposite, with satisfaction levels falling from 44.4% in late 2004 to 29.3% at the end of 2005. Satisfaction with police assistance was highest in the RS (66.3%), up on the final quarter of the previous year, when it was just 51.3%. It is worth noting that in all quarters women expressed more satisfaction with police response. (Table IX).

It is important to note that members of the local minority and majority groups were equally likely to be victims of crime in all three majority areas, and that there is no notable difference in the demand for police assistance between the local minority and majority populations in any of the majority areas. The level of satisfaction with police assistance was lower at the end of 2005 than it was in 2004 in all three majority areas, but this is not the case with the majority samples in the various areas. In fact, on the basis of our surveys, there does not appear to a direct relationship between crime and ethnic discrimination in any of the three majority areas of BiH. (Table IX).

We also note the high percentage who think the police are too soft on threats to public safety. Such criticism is rising in all three majority areas. (Table XI).

More people also said they had experienced or seen the abuse of police powers some time during the previous six months. The level has consistently been highest in Croat majority areas: 18.9% in the final

Table XII
Witnessed or experienced the abuse of police authorities during the previous six months

	Total		Bosniak majority areas		Croat majority areas		Serb majority areas	
Survey	04/#4	05/#4	04/#4	05/#4	04/#4	05#4	04/#4	05#4
In %	5.1	7.2	2.7	6.3	13.2	18.9	5.6	4.8
Index 05/#4 - 04/#4	141.2		233.3		143.2		85.7	

Source: Opinion poll carried out for EWS by PRISM Research

II Institutional stability in BiH - Tables

Table Ia
Do you approve of the work of....?

Sample	All				Gender							
					Men				Women			
	Feb 05.	Jun 05.	Sep 05.	Nov 05.	Feb 05.	Jun 05.	Sep 05.	Nov 05.	Feb 05.	Jun 05.	Sep 05.	Nov 05.
	%	%	%	%	%	%	%	%	%	%	%	%
BiH Presidency												
Yes	42.0	41.0	38.1	40.4	41.2	40.3	39.5	40.8	42.8	41.7	36.7	40.1
No	36.4	41.6	44.6	41.3	40.3	44.2	45.9	42.8	32.5	39.2	43.3	39.7
Not applicable	2.0	1.3	1.3	0.9	1.4	1.6	1.1	0.7	2.5	1.1	1.6	1.1
Neither approve nor disapprove	12.5	8.9	9.5	9.8	11.3	8.0	8.0	9.5	13.6	9.9	11.0	10.0
DK/NA	7.1	7.1	6.5	7.6	5.7	6.0	5.6	6.1	8.4	8.1	7.4	9.1
Total	100.0	100.0	100.0	100.0	100.0	100.0	100.0	100.0	100.0	100.0	100.0	100.0
BiH Parliament												
Yes	42.0	42.5	38.1	38.9	40.9	42.4	39.9	39.0	43.1	42.6	36.4	38.8
No	36.5	40.5	45.1	41.7	41.2	43.0	46.1	44.1	32.0	38.1	44.0	39.4
Not applicable	1.7	0.4	0.6	1.2	1.1	0.3	0.5	0.9	2.4	0.5	0.7	1.5
Neither approve nor disapprove	11.7	8.4	9.7	10.3	9.8	7.3	7.8	10.0	13.5	9.5	11.5	10.7
DK/NA	8.1	8.2	6.5	8.0	7.1	7.1	5.7	6.1	9.0	9.2	7.4	9.7
Total	100.0	100.0	100.0	100.0	100.0	100.0	100.0	100.0	100.0	100.0	100.0	100.0
Council of Ministers												
Yes	42.2	42.9	39.9	38.2	42.5	43.0	42.7	38.7	42.0	42.7	37.3	37.7
No	37.0	39.7	44.2	42.1	40.3	42.2	44.4	44.3	33.9	37.3	44.0	40.0
Not applicable	2.0	0.4	0.8	1.3	1.7	0.3	0.8	1.0	2.2	0.6	0.7	1.6
Neither approve nor disapprove	10.8	8.4	9.2	10.6	8.6	6.9	7.1	10.0	12.9	9.9	11.2	11.1
DK/NA	8.0	8.6	5.9	7.8	7.0	7.6	5.0	6.0	9.0	9.5	6.9	9.5
Total	100.0	100.0	100.0	100.0	100.0	100.0	100.0	100.0	100.0	100.0	100.0	100.0
FBiH Parliament												
Yes	39.2	40.0	39.2	36.3	38.0	40.8	40.8	36.0	40.3	39.3	37.6	36.5
No	37.2	36.9	44.1	41.9	41.2	38.8	45.4	44.4	33.3	35.1	42.8	39.5
Not applicable	1.6	3.9	0.7	1.5	1.5	3.6	0.6	0.7	1.7	4.2	0.7	2.2
Neither approve nor disapprove	11.1	8.7	9.5	11.4	9.8	7.9	7.0	11.2	12.3	9.5	11.8	11.6
DK/NA	11.0	10.5	6.6	9.0	9.5	8.9	6.2	7.8	12.4	12.0	7.1	10.2
Total	100.0	100.0	100.0	100.0	100.0	100.0	100.0	100.0	100.0	100.0	100.0	100.0
FBiH Government												
Yes	40.3	39.5	39.7	37.6	38.6	41.0	42.3	37.6	42.0	38.0	37.2	37.5
No	36.6	38.0	43.5	40.9	40.9	39.5	44.3	43.0	32.5	36.5	42.6	38.9
Not applicable	1.4	4.2	0.8	1.3	1.1	3.6	0.6	0.8	1.6	4.8	1.1	1.8
Neither approve nor disapprove	10.5	8.2	9.4	11.4	9.4	7.6	6.6	10.9	11.6	8.8	12.0	11.9
DK/NA	11.2	10.2	6.7	8.8	9.9	8.3	6.2	7.7	12.4	12.0	7.1	9.9
Total	100.0	100.0	100.0	100.0	100.0	100.0	100.0	100.0	100.0	100.0	100.0	100.0
RS National Assembly												
Yes	37.7	32.3	30.3	32.5	35.4	32.1	33.3	33.0	39.9	32.4	27.3	31.9
No	41.6	46.2	49.2	46.4	46.5	47.1	48.4	47.1	36.9	45.4	50.0	45.8
Not applicable	1.0	1.3	2.2	2.4	0.5	1.9	2.7	1.9	1.4	0.8	1.8	2.9
Neither approve nor disapprove	9.5	9.3	10.9	10.4	7.4	8.1	9.4	10.5	11.4	10.5	12.4	10.4
DK/NA	10.3	10.9	7.3	8.3	10.2	10.8	6.2	7.5	10.3	10.9	8.5	9.0
Total	100.0	100.0	100.0	100.0	100.0	100.0	100.0	100.0	100.0	100.0	100.0	100.0
RS Government												
Yes	37.5	32.4	30.6	32.5	35.3	32.5	34.1	32.6	39.7	32.2	27.3	32.4
No	41.9	46.4	48.9	46.5	46.1	47.7	47.7	47.7	37.8	45.2	50.1	45.3
Not applicable	1.0	1.2	2.2	2.4	0.4	1.4	2.7	1.9	1.5	1.0	1.7	2.9
Neither approve nor disapprove	9.8	9.4	10.9	10.6	8.4	8.3	9.2	10.7	11.2	10.5	12.5	10.6
DK/NA	9.7	10.6	7.4	8.0	9.7	10.2	6.3	7.1	9.8	11.0	8.4	8.8
Total	100.0	100.0	100.0	100.0	100.0	100.0	100.0	100.0	100.0	100.0	100.0	100.0
Municipal authorities												
Yes	52.9	50.4	45.6	51.3	51.7	53.0	49.1	51.9	54.0	47.9	42.2	50.7
No	30.2	32.3	39.4	31.8	33.4	31.8	37.8	34.3	27.1	32.7	41.0	29.4
Not applicable	1.0	0.3	0.8	1.4	0.4	0.2	1.1	0.8	1.6	0.4	0.5	1.9
Neither approve nor disapprove	9.0	8.8	8.2	9.8	7.6	8.3	6.7	9.2	10.3	9.3	9.6	10.4
DK/NA	7.1	8.3	5.9	5.7	7.0	6.7	5.3	3.8	7.1	9.8	6.6	7.6
Total	100.0	100.0	100.0	100.0	100.0	100.0	100.0	100.0	100.0	100.0	100.0	100.0

53

Table Ib
Do you approve of the work of....?

Sample	All				Men				Women			
	Feb 05. %	Jun 05. %	Sep 05. %	Nov 05. %	Feb 05. %	Jun 05. %	Sep 05. %	Nov 05. %	Feb 05. %	Jun 05. %	Sep 05. %	Nov 05. %
OSCE												
Yes	46.1	48.5	40.8	42.2	42.7	50.7	44.2	43.0	49.4	46.3	37.6	41.4
No	34.2	32.4	38.5	33.7	39.1	33.7	37.3	34.5	29.6	31.2	39.6	32.9
Not applicable	1.0	0.6	0.8	1.0	1.3	0.5	0.8	0.6	0.7	0.8	0.8	1.4
Neither approve nor disapprove	9.2	8.6	13.0	12.8	7.8	7.1	12.0	12.7	10.5	10.1	13.9	12.9
DK/NA	9.4	9.8	7.0	10.3	9.2	8.0	5.7	9.2	9.7	11.6	8.2	11.4
Total	100.0	100.0	100.0	100.0	100.0	100.0	100.0	100.0	100.0	100.0	100.0	100.0
OHR												
Yes	42.1	44.0	37.5	38.1	38.8	44.1	40.0	39.0	45.2	43.8	35.1	37.2
No	39.9	38.0	41.9	38.1	45.7	40.8	41.8	39.0	34.2	35.3	42.0	37.2
Not applicable	1.1	0.7	1.2	0.9	0.9	0.4	1.5	0.3	1.4	0.9	0.9	1.5
Neither approve nor disapprove	8.4	8.4	11.8	12.9	6.7	6.6	10.3	13.9	10.0	10.1	13.3	11.9
DK/NA	8.5	9.0	7.6	10.0	7.9	8.2	6.4	7.7	9.1	9.9	8.7	12.2
Total	100.0	100.0	100.0	100.0	100.0	100.0	100.0	100.0	100.0	100.0	100.0	100.0
UNDP												
Yes	43.0	46.6	40.2	41.6	39.7	47.9	44.8	43.1	46.1	45.3	35.8	40.2
No	32.6	31.1	39.0	32.1	38.4	32.6	37.2	32.1	27.1	29.6	40.7	32.2
Not applicable	1.4	0.7	1.5	1.1	1.4	0.4	1.1	0.6	1.3	0.9	1.9	1.6
Neither approve nor disapprove	9.1	8.1	11.0	12.9	7.3	6.5	9.4	13.2	10.8	9.6	12.5	12.6
DK/NA	14.0	13.6	8.3	12.3	13.2	12.6	7.5	11.0	14.7	14.6	9.1	13.5
Total	100.0	100.0	100.0	100.0	100.0	100.0	100.0	100.0	100.0	100.0	100.0	100.0
SFOR/EUFOR												
Yes	42.4	44.4	38.4	40.4	41.0	45.8	41.9	40.7	43.7	43.1	35.0	40.1
No	37.3	35.8	42.7	35.8	41.0	36.1	42.2	36.7	33.7	35.6	43.2	35.0
Not applicable	1.5	0.6	1.0	1.2	1.8	0.6	0.9	0.7	1.2	0.7	1.1	1.7
Neither approve nor disapprove	9.7	8.8	10.9	13.1	8.4	7.4	9.3	13.5	10.9	10.1	12.5	12.8
DK/NA	9.1	10.3	7.0	9.5	7.7	10.1	5.7	8.5	10.5	10.5	8.2	10.4
Total	100.0	100.0	100.0	100.0	100.0	100.0	100.0	100.0	100.0	100.0	100.0	100.0
EU												
Yes	48.8	49.1	43.0	47.0	45.7	51.2	47.8	47.7	51.7	47.1	38.5	46.3
No	31.9	32.4	38.4	29.5	37.2	31.7	36.3	30.6	26.7	33.1	40.3	28.3
Not applicable	1.2	0.7	0.9	1.0	1.4	0.7	0.8	0.5	1.0	0.6	1.0	1.4
Neither approve nor disapprove	9.4	7.9	11.0	12.9	7.5	6.5	9.5	13.1	11.1	9.3	12.5	12.7
DK/NA	8.8	9.9	6.6	9.7	8.1	9.9	5.6	8.0	9.5	9.9	7.7	11.2
Total	100.0	100.0	100.0	100.0	100.0	100.0	100.0	100.0	100.0	100.0	100.0	100.0
US												
Yes	33.8	35.5	31.0	33.9	30.9	36.2	33.5	33.6	36.6	34.9	28.6	34.2
No	47.5	46.7	49.3	42.3	52.0	47.8	49.6	44.8	43.2	45.7	48.9	39.9
Not applicable	0.9	0.7	1.1	1.0	1.1	0.6	0.9	0.6	0.7	0.8	1.2	1.3
Neither approve nor disapprove	8.5	7.9	12.3	13.0	6.9	7.0	10.9	12.5	10.0	8.8	13.7	13.5
DK/NA	9.3	9.2	6.3	9.9	9.1	8.4	5.0	8.6	9.5	9.9	7.6	11.2
Total	100.0	100.0	100.0	100.0	100.0	100.0	100.0	100.0	100.0	100.0	100.0	100.0

Table IIa
Do you approve of the work of....?

Sample	Bosniak majority areas				Croat majority areas				Serb majority areas			
	Feb 05.	Jun 05.	Sep 05.	Nov 05.	Feb 05.	Jun 05.	Sep 05.	Nov 05.	Feb 05.	Jun 05.	Sep 05.	Nov 05.
	%	%	%	%	%	%	%	%	%	%	%	%
BiH Presidency												
Yes	48.3	44.5	37.8	40.6	33.0	42.9	41.0	36.9	37.6	37.3	37.8	39.5
No	35.4	35.1	45.2	41.9	23.3	32.2	26.6	36.0	41.2	50.9	48.7	43.1
Not applicable	1.5	1.7	1.5	1.0	4.5	1.9	1.2	1.6	1.7	0.8	1.2	0.6
Neither approve nor disapprove	9.3	9.8	9.4	9.3	26.1	11.7	16.7	16.0	12.4	7.4	7.7	8.8
DK/NA	5.5	8.8	6.1	7.2	13.0	11.3	14.5	9.5	7.2	3.7	4.5	7.9
Total	100.0	100.0	100.0	100.0	100.0	100.0	100.0	100.0	100.0	100.0	100.0	100.0
BiH Parliament												
Yes	49.3	48.2	38.7	40.3	31.3	39.8	40.9	33.6	36.8	37.0	36.8	37.0
No	35.2	33.2	45.8	41.2	23.7	34.8	27.4	34.4	41.9	50.2	49.1	45.6
Not applicable	1.5	0.2	0.1	1.0	5.1	1.9	0.6	3.2	1.1	0.2	1.2	0.8
Neither approve nor disapprove	8.1	9.5	9.8	9.8	25.0	12.2	16.0	19.5	11.9	6.2	7.9	8.4
DK/NA	6.0	8.9	5.5	7.7	14.9	11.3	15.1	9.3	8.3	6.5	5.1	8.2
Total	100.0	100.0	100.0	100.0	100.0	100.0	100.0	100.0	100.0	100.0	100.0	100.0
Council of Ministers												
Yes	49.1	47.8	42.0	39.2	31.8	37.7	41.1	32.9	37.5	38.2	36.8	36.9
No	35.2	34.1	44.4	41.7	24.1	36.3	25.8	34.0	42.5	47.4	49.7	46.2
Not applicable	1.9		0.1	1.0	5.3	2.4	1.7	4.1	1.1	0.3	1.2	0.8
Neither approve nor disapprove	7.8	9.4	8.2	10.2	24.3	11.8	17.1	20.0	10.4	6.6	8.2	8.4
DK/NA	6.0	8.7	5.2	7.8	14.5	11.8	14.3	9.0	8.4	7.5	4.1	7.8
Total	100.0	100.0	100.0	100.0	100.0	100.0	100.0	100.0	100.0	100.0	100.0	100.0
FBiH Parliament												
Yes	49.0	47.6	43.6	39.2	31.0	42.5	38.3	32.1	30.2	30.3	34.6	32.7
No	35.7	33.2	42.2	41.2	24.7	31.4	28.3	33.5	42.3	42.3	50.5	46.3
Not applicable	1.1		0.1	1.0	5.3	2.4	1.0	6.3	1.1	9.1	1.2	0.4
Neither approve nor disapprove	8.5	10.2	8.8	11.1	24.2	11.8	17.8	19.0	10.3	6.5	8.0	9.4
DK/NA	5.6	9.0	5.2	7.5	14.8	12.0	14.6	9.0	16.2	11.8	5.7	11.2
Total	100.0	100.0	100.0	100.0	100.0	100.0	100.0	100.0	100.0	100.0	100.0	100.0
FBiH Government												
Yes	50.8	48.4	45.1	41.6	32.6	42.3	39.8	32.6	30.3	28.3	34.6	33.0
No	35.8	33.1	40.8	39.1	23.8	31.1	27.8	32.0	41.3	45.0	50.2	46.5
Not applicable	0.6	0.2	0.2	1.0	5.1	2.4	1.0	5.1	1.1	9.6	1.2	0.4
Neither approve nor disapprove	7.7	9.2	8.5	10.5	23.9	11.8	17.3	20.3	9.9	6.2	8.3	10.1
DK/NA	5.0	9.1	5.4	7.8	14.6	12.4	14.1	10.0	17.4	10.9	5.8	9.9
Total	100.0	100.0	100.0	100.0	100.0	100.0	100.0	100.0	100.0	100.0	100.0	100.0
RS National Assembly												
Yes	28.4	18.1	20.2	16.3	21.0	31.6	21.8	21.7	53.3	48.8	46.1	55.8
No	53.0	51.6	56.0	59.2	28.7	38.9	40.3	36.7	32.7	41.5	42.3	32.7
Not applicable	0.4	2.1	4.1	1.9	4.5	2.3	1.1	11.1	0.5	0.2	0.4	0.2
Neither approve nor disapprove	8.4	12.0	12.2	11.8	21.0	11.8	20.4	16.4	7.3	6.0	6.9	7.4
DK/NA	9.8	16.1	7.6	10.7	24.9	15.4	16.4	14.1	6.3	3.6	4.3	3.9
Total	100.0	100.0	100.0	100.0	100.0	100.0	100.0	100.0	100.0	100.0	100.0	100.0
RS Government												
Yes	28.0	17.4	19.6	16.5	21.6	33.9	21.3	21.0	53.6	49.1	47.8	55.9
No	53.1	52.4	57.3	58.6	28.7	37.0	39.6	36.0	32.9	41.8	40.3	33.7
Not applicable	0.5	2.2	4.0	1.8	5.1	1.8	1.1	12.1	0.2		0.4	
Neither approve nor disapprove	8.7	12.6	11.4	11.9	21.7	12.2	20.6	16.5	7.7	5.4	7.6	7.8
DK/NA	9.8	15.5	7.7	11.2	22.9	15.1	17.3	14.4	5.7	3.7	3.9	2.6
Total	100.0	100.0	100.0	100.0	100.0	100.0	100.0	100.0	100.0	100.0	100.0	100.0
Municipal authorities												
Yes	54.7	55.1	45.2	49.8	41.1	39.4	37.7	39.2	54.5	49.3	48.9	55.7
No	32.1	27.3	41.3	31.7	19.5	32.2	28.8	29.6	31.3	37.0	40.5	33.5
Not applicable	0.8		0.9	1.0	3.5	0.8	0.8	6.8	0.2	0.5	0.4	
Neither approve nor disapprove	7.1	8.3	7.4	9.8	20.1	14.4	17.6	17.2	7.8	7.9	6.4	7.8
DK/NA	5.3	9.4	5.3	7.7	15.8	13.2	15.2	8.1	6.3	5.3	3.8	3.0
Total	100.0	100.0	100.0	100.0	100.0	100.0	100.0	100.0	100.0	100.0	100.0	100.0

55

134

Table IIb
Do you approve of the work of....?

Sample	Bosniak majority areas				Croat majority areas				Serb majority areas			
	Feb 05.	Jun 05.	Sep 05.	Nov 05.	Feb 05.	Jun 05.	Sep 05.	Nov 05.	Feb 05.	Jun 05.	Sep 05.	Nov 05.
	%	%	%	%	%	%	%	%	%	%	%	%
Cantonal Authorities												
Yes	55.4	54.2	44.3	44.8	38.0	42.2	39.8	37.1				
No	32.6	26.6	42.5	34.5	21.5	28.9	24.8	28.8				
Not applicable	0.2	0.2	0.4	1.0	3.3	0.8	0.6	6.6				
Neither approve nor disapprove	6.9	9.5	7.3	12.0	19.6	15.0	19.0	18.0				
DK/NA	4.8	9.5	5.5	7.7	17.7	13.2	15.9	9.6				
Total	100.0	100.0	100.0	100.0	100.0	100.0	100.0	100.0				
OSCE												
Yes	50.1	52.2	46.2	44.4	40.0	53.2	41.2	42.7	43.7	42.1	35.0	38.8
No	32.2	25.4	33.0	28.4	19.4	25.4	23.1	25.7	40.5	42.9	49.4	42.9
Not applicable	0.8	0.4	0.4	0.8	3.3	0.8	0.6	3.0	0.6	1.0	0.4	0.3
Neither approve nor disapprove	8.4	11.7	14.8	13.4	19.6	8.0	19.4	16.1	7.2	5.6	9.4	11.3
DK/NA	8.5	10.4	5.7	13.0	17.8	12.7	15.7	12.4	8.1	8.4	5.8	6.8
Total	100.0	100.0	100.0	100.0	100.0	100.0	100.0	100.0	100.0	100.0	100.0	100.0
OHR												
Yes	53.8	49.5	48.2	42.7	35.9	50.8	31.0	40.7	31.6	35.6	27.8	32.0
No	30.4	29.4	30.6	29.3	23.7	27.2	33.6	30.6	55.2	50.9	57.1	50.7
Not applicable	0.5	0.4	1.8	0.8	2.6	0.5	0.8	3.3	1.0	0.9	0.4	0.2
Neither approve nor disapprove	7.4	10.8	13.0	15.4	20.5	8.1	18.2	14.8	5.8	6.0	8.4	9.7
DK/NA	7.9	9.9	6.4	11.9	17.3	13.4	16.5	10.6	6.5	6.6	6.3	7.5
Total	100.0	100.0	100.0	100.0	100.0	100.0	100.0	100.0	100.0	100.0	100.0	100.0
UNDP												
Yes	48.3	53.8	45.8	41.3	41.7	53.6	41.3	46.5	37.7	36.3	33.8	40.1
No	32.8	22.2	32.0	29.4	16.2	23.0	24.7	20.7	36.8	43.4	51.9	39.1
Not applicable	1.1	0.2	1.8	0.8	3.6	1.3	0.6	4.0	1.0	0.8	0.4	0.3
Neither approve nor disapprove	8.6	11.5	12.8	13.4	18.9	9.0	17.8	15.7	6.6	4.2	6.9	12.0
DK/NA	9.2	12.3	7.6	15.1	19.5	13.1	15.6	13.1	18.0	15.3	7.0	8.5
Total	100.0	100.0	100.0	100.0	100.0	100.0	100.0	100.0	100.0	100.0	100.0	100.0
SFOR/EUFOR												
Yes	53.1	49.8	47.5	45.8	37.2	52.3	36.6	40.7	33.0	35.5	28.3	33.5
No	28.8	26.6	33.0	27.6	22.3	25.3	30.3	31.4	50.6	50.4	58.4	47.4
Not applicable	1.1	0.2	1.2	1.0	3.1	0.8	0.6	4.2	1.4	0.7	0.4	0.3
Neither approve nor disapprove	8.4	13.0	12.6	14.6	19.7	8.1	16.9	13.5	8.0	4.1	7.0	11.9
DK/NA	8.6	10.4	5.7	11.1	17.7	13.5	15.6	10.2	7.0	9.3	5.8	7.0
Total	100.0	100.0	100.0	100.0	100.0	100.0	100.0	100.0	100.0	100.0	100.0	100.0
EU												
Yes	54.9	54.4	50.0	46.8	45.3	48.9	40.5	53.6	44.3	43.4	36.4	44.8
No	27.7	22.8	31.4	27.3	15.0	27.8	24.7	18.1	40.8	45.1	50.7	35.9
Not applicable	0.9	0.2	0.4	0.9	2.6	0.8	0.9	2.7	1.0	0.8	0.8	0.3
Neither approve nor disapprove	8.4	11.6	12.5	13.8	19.3	8.1	18.3	15.7	7.1	3.6	7.3	11.5
DK/NA	8.1	11.0	5.8	11.2	17.7	14.5	15.6	9.9	6.8	7.1	4.8	7.5
Total	100.0	100.0	100.0	100.0	100.0	100.0	100.0	100.0	100.0	100.0	100.0	100.0
US												
Yes	43.5	39.9	36.7	35.7	36.0	44.9	32.1	44.0	22.7	26.9	24.3	27.6
No	37.7	37.1	43.0	34.4	22.5	32.4	32.1	29.0	66.1	63.3	62.5	56.4
Not applicable	0.9	0.4	1.0	0.8	2.6	0.8	0.9	3.2	0.4	0.6	0.4	0.2
Neither approve nor disapprove	7.6	11.6	13.9	17.1	20.6	8.0	19.1	13.7	5.3	3.6	8.6	8.6
DK/NA	10.3	10.9	5.5	12.0	18.3	13.9	15.8	10.1	5.5	5.6	4.1	7.2
Total	100.0	100.0	100.0	100.0	100.0	100.0	100.0	100.0	100.0	100.0	100.0	100.0

Table IIIa

How widespread do you think corruption understood as taking bribes and abuse of office for peronsal gain in the following institions

Sample	All				Men				Women			
	Feb 05.	Jun 05.	Sep 05.	Nov 05.	Feb 05.	Jun 05.	Sep 05.	Nov 05.	Feb 05.	Jun 05.	Sep 05.	Nov 05.
	%	%	%	%	%	%	%	%	%	%	%	%
BiH Presidency												
Not at all	1.7	2.9	2.0	3.8	2.0	3.1	1.9	4.6	1.4	2.7	2.1	3.0
A little	18.7	18.2	16.6	14.9	18.4	19.6	13.3	13.6	19.0	16.9	20.0	16.2
Moderately	17.4	17.0	18.5	26.6	13.4	16.2	19.5	26.1	21.4	17.6	17.5	27.1
Fairly	26.9	23.9	20.5	24.4	27.9	21.3	23.0	22.8	25.9	26.4	18.0	26.1
Very	35.3	38.0	42.4	30.3	38.2	39.8	42.3	33.0	32.4	36.3	42.5	27.7
Total	100.0	100.0	100.0	100.0	100.0	100.0	100.0	100.0	100.0	100.0	100.0	100.0
BiH Parliament												
Not at all	1.5	2.3	1.9	3.7	1.9	2.4	2.0	4.0	1.0	2.1	1.9	3.5
A little	16.6	18.1	16.4	14.5	17.2	18.8	12.5	12.6	16.0	17.4	20.3	16.4
Moderately	18.2	18.6	18.7	24.5	13.9	17.6	19.8	23.5	22.5	19.6	17.7	25.4
Fairly	28.9	25.9	22.9	27.0	28.9	23.9	25.7	26.6	28.9	27.8	20.1	27.4
Very	34.8	35.2	40.1	30.3	38.0	37.3	40.1	33.4	31.6	33.1	40.1	27.3
Total	100.0	100.0	100.0	100.0	100.0	100.0	100.0	100.0	100.0	100.0	100.0	100.0
Council of Ministers												
Not at all	1.1	2.3	2.4	3.4	1.2	2.9	2.9	3.4	1.0	1.8	2.0	3.3
A little	17.0	17.1	15.9	14.9	17.6	18.6	12.3	13.5	16.5	15.6	19.4	16.4
Moderately	18.1	18.0	16.7	24.4	14.4	15.9	18.0	24.1	21.8	19.9	15.4	24.7
Fairly	28.0	26.6	23.5	25.6	27.8	23.4	24.6	23.6	28.1	29.8	22.4	27.6
Very	35.7	36.0	41.6	31.7	39.0	39.2	42.3	35.4	32.6	32.9	40.8	27.9
Total	100.0	100.0	100.0	100.0	100.0	100.0	100.0	100.0	100.0	100.0	100.0	100.0
FBiH Parliament												
Not at all	2.2	2.3	1.5	3.4	2.8	2.4	1.7	3.4	1.5	2.2	1.3	3.4
A little	16.1	18.6	15.9	14.7	15.3	20.4	12.4	12.4	17.0	16.8	19.3	16.9
Moderately	17.2	17.6	18.9	25.3	12.3	16.4	20.7	25.0	22.1	18.8	17.1	25.7
Fairly	27.6	25.6	22.2	25.5	28.4	21.9	23.4	25.2	26.8	29.2	21.0	25.8
Very	36.9	35.9	41.5	31.1	41.2	38.9	41.8	33.9	32.5	32.9	41.2	28.2
Total	100.0	100.0	100.0	100.0	100.0	100.0	100.0	100.0	100.0	100.0	100.0	100.0
FBiH Government												
Not at all	1.4	2.1	1.8	3.1	2.1	2.7	1.8	3.4	0.8	1.4	1.8	2.9
A little	15.6	18.2	15.5	14.8	15.1	19.3	12.3	14.2	16.1	17.2	18.7	15.4
Moderately	18.6	17.0	17.6	24.9	13.1	14.5	18.9	23.5	24.0	19.3	16.3	26.3
Fairly	26.2	26.5	22.7	25.2	26.6	26.0	24.6	24.4	25.8	27.1	20.7	26.0
Very	38.2	36.2	42.4	32.0	43.1	37.5	42.3	34.5	33.3	35.0	42.5	29.4
Total	100.0	100.0	100.0	100.0	100.0	100.0	100.0	100.0	100.0	100.0	100.0	100.0
RS National Assembly												
Not at all	1.6	1.7	1.2	2.7	1.8	1.8	1.3	3.0	1.4	1.6	1.1	2.4
A little	12.2	13.2	13.6	13.8	10.7	14.3	11.0	13.0	13.7	12.2	16.0	14.6
Moderately	21.1	17.1	16.7	21.6	17.9	15.0	15.7	19.9	24.2	19.2	17.6	23.3
Fairly	26.4	27.3	22.6	27.4	28.0	24.7	23.7	26.9	24.9	29.9	21.6	27.9
Very	38.7	40.6	45.9	34.6	41.5	44.2	48.3	37.3	35.9	37.1	43.6	31.9
Total	100.0	100.0	100.0	100.0	100.0	100.0	100.0	100.0	100.0	100.0	100.0	100.0
RS Government												
Not at all	1.9	2.0	1.3	3.0	2.5	2.3	1.5	3.0	1.4	1.7	1.1	2.9
A little	11.6	12.7	13.6	13.5	12.2	14.3	10.9	12.1	11.0	11.1	16.2	14.9
Moderately	18.9	17.5	15.6	20.8	14.5	14.5	13.8	20.4	23.3	20.5	17.4	21.2
Fairly	28.5	25.7	22.1	27.2	28.4	24.2	23.9	27.1	28.5	27.1	20.3	27.3
Very	39.1	42.1	47.4	35.6	42.5	44.7	49.8	37.4	35.8	39.6	45.0	33.8
Total	100.0	100.0	100.0	100.0	100.0	100.0	100.0	100.0	100.0	100.0	100.0	100.0

Table IIIb
How widespread do you think corruption understood as taking bribes and abuse of office for peronsal gain in the following institionts

Sample	All				Men				Women			
	Feb 05.	Jun 05.	Sep 05.	Nov 05.	Feb 05.	Jun 05.	Sep 05.	Nov 05.	Feb 05.	Jun 05.	Sep 05.	Nov 05.
	%	%	%	%	%	%	%	%	%	%	%	%
Municipal authorities												
Not at all	1.2	3.1	1.9	5.2	1.1	3.1	2.4	4.7	1.2	3.2	1.5	5.8
A little	15.7	18.7	16.0	20.4	15.1	19.2	13.4	20.3	16.2	18.1	18.6	20.6
Moderately	23.8	17.8	19.6	20.6	20.5	17.6	20.4	18.5	27.0	18.0	18.7	22.6
Fairly	28.5	24.8	21.9	23.0	30.3	23.7	21.9	23.7	26.8	25.9	21.8	22.3
Very	30.9	35.6	40.6	30.8	33.0	36.5	41.8	32.9	28.9	34.8	39.5	28.8
Total	100.0	100.0	100.0	100.0	100.0	100.0	100.0	100.0	100.0	100.0	100.0	100.0
OSCE												
Not at all	12.0	13.0	6.6	11.3	11.1	16.6	7.3	11.0	13.0	9.4	5.8	11.7
A little	17.7	20.5	18.4	21.0	19.5	18.9	18.6	22.3	15.9	22.1	18.2	19.6
Moderately	21.2	21.2	18.5	21.2	17.1	20.6	18.9	21.4	25.3	21.9	18.2	21.0
Fairly	21.6	20.6	20.4	21.6	22.2	20.0	19.7	19.6	21.0	21.3	21.2	23.6
Very	27.5	24.7	36.1	24.9	30.1	24.0	35.5	25.7	25.0	25.3	36.6	24.1
Total	100.0	100.0	100.0	100.0	100.0	100.0	100.0	100.0	100.0	100.0	100.0	100.0
OHR												
Not at all	10.3	13.5	6.1	11.1	8.4	17.9	6.6	9.7	12.2	8.9	5.6	12.5
A little	18.6	20.1	17.2	21.8	20.5	18.5	15.9	23.8	16.6	21.7	18.6	19.9
Moderately	22.5	21.2	19.0	20.6	20.1	19.5	19.8	21.7	24.9	22.9	18.1	19.5
Fairly	21.3	20.2	20.5	20.8	22.3	20.6	18.4	20.4	20.4	20.5	20.5	23.3
Very	27.3	25.0	37.2	25.6	28.7	25.6	37.1	26.4	25.9	24.5	37.2	24.8
Total	100.0	100.0	100.0	100.0	100.0	100.0	100.0	100.0	100.0	100.0	100.0	100.0
UNDP												
Not at all	11.9	15.4	7.7	12.9	10.7	20.7	7.9	12.0	13.1	10.1	7.5	13.7
A little	17.1	21.9	19.7	22.5	18.0	20.6	19.0	25.0	16.3	23.3	20.5	19.9
Moderately	23.0	19.9	18.1	21.4	20.8	17.0	18.6	22.3	25.2	22.8	17.6	20.5
Fairly	20.1	19.5	18.4	18.8	20.5	18.2	18.3	15.9	19.8	20.8	18.5	21.7
Very	27.8	23.3	36.1	24.5	30.0	23.4	36.2	24.8	25.6	23.1	36.0	24.2
Total	100.0	100.0	100.0	100.0	100.0	100.0	100.0	100.0	100.0	100.0	100.0	100.0
EU												
Not at all	15.6	16.1	7.6	16.1	14.6	21.3	8.1	14.5	16.6	10.8	7.1	17.7
A little	17.6	21.7	21.1	22.5	20.1	19.8	20.1	25.0	15.2	23.8	22.1	19.9
Moderately	21.6	19.5	17.0	19.8	17.0	16.9	17.1	20.8	26.1	22.0	16.9	18.7
Fairly	20.4	19.3	18.4	18.8	21.6	18.0	18.5	16.1	19.3	20.6	18.3	21.6
Very	24.7	23.4	35.9	22.9	26.7	24.0	36.2	23.7	22.8	22.8	35.6	22.1
Total	100.0	100.0	100.0	100.0	100.0	100.0	100.0	100.0	100.0	100.0	100.0	100.0

III ECONOMIC STABILITY IN BOSNIA AND HERZEGOVINA

The Economic Stability Index

The Economic Stability Index is based on opinion poll results, covering both the general public and the business sector. It reflects the opinion of these groups regarding the current and future economic environment in Bosnia and Herzegovina. In contrast to earlier years, the chain and composite indices saw significant change during 2005. The chain index fluctuated, but the composite index fell steadily, reaching its lowest value in five years of monitoring.

Economic Stability Index for BiH

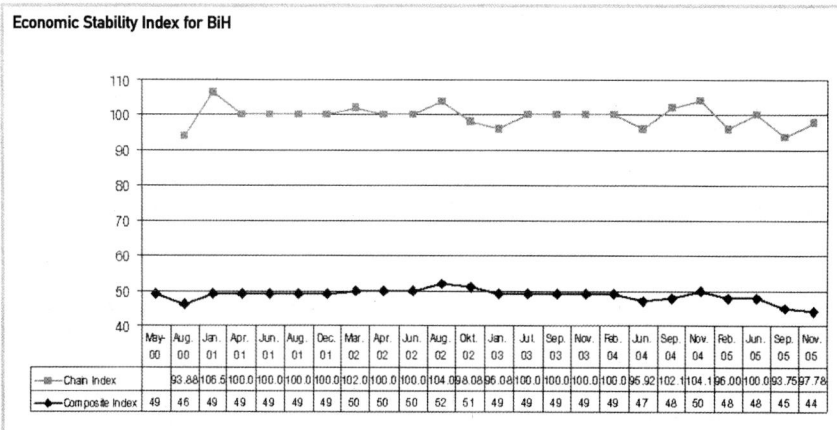

	May. 00	Aug. 00	Jan. 01	Apr. 01	Jun. 01	Aug. 01	Dec. 01	Mar. 02	Apr. 02	Jun. 02	Aug. 02	Okt. 02	Jan. 03	Jul. 03	Sep. 03	Nov. 03	Feb. 04	Jun. 04	Sep. 04	Nov. 04	Feb. 05	Jun. 05	Sep. 05	Nov. 05
Chain Index	93.88	105.5	100.0	100.0	100.0	100.0	100.0	102.0	100.0	100.0	104.09	8.08	96.08	100.0	100.0	100.0	100.0	95.92	102.1	104.1	96.00	100.0	93.75	97.78
Composite Index	49	46	49	49	49	49	49	50	50	50	52	51	49	49	49	49	47	48	50	48	48	45	44

Both our opinion polls reveal a worsening situation, particularly during the second half of 2005. The worst results were recorded during the last quarterly survey of the year. While it is difficult to ascertain all the reasons for these trends in public opinion, one is certainly the introduction of VAT. As the date of VAT introduction approached, the public became increasingly concerned. Our poll results show a clear majority expressing fear of price hikes and falling income. This certainly promoted a more negative approach to the economic situation.

1. Industrial production

Industrial production rose in both entities of BiH during 2005, though more in the RS than in the FBiH.

The indices of the volume of industrial production, compared to the same month the previous year, differed considerably between the entities. It was lowest during the first two months of 2005 and peaked during the summer. The RS index was particularly high in June and July, at 140 and has generally been above 100.

In the FBiH, industrial production increased most in the following branches: coke, oil derivatives, and nuclear fuel, followed by motor vehicles, trailers, and semi-trailers, and in third place metal ore extraction.[1]

---

1   The values of the indices were respectively: 211.5; 208.7; and 189.9. Source: Federal Statistics Office, February 2006.   19

138

Graph 1: The volume of industrial production for 2005

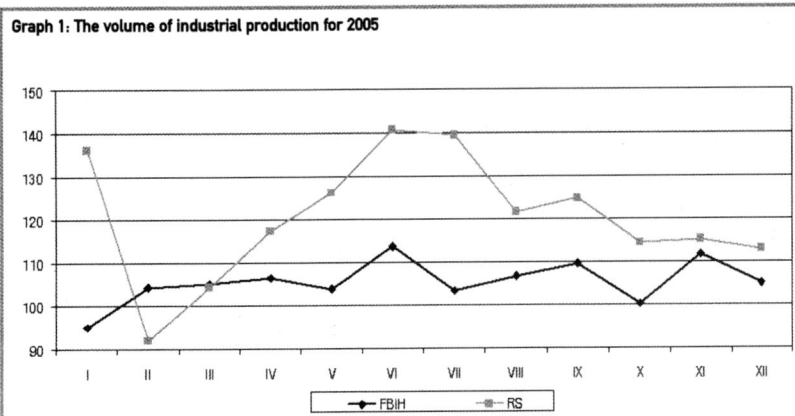

In the RS, it rose most in the following three sectors: leather, leather goods, and shoes, followed by other electrical machines and devices, and by radio, TV and communications equipment.[2]

FBiH production contracted most with regard to medical, precise, and optical instruments and timepieces, followed by publishing and printing, and finally clothes and furs.[3] In the RS, it was lowest with regard to the production of other machines and devices, wood and cork processing and products, and other mineral products.[4]

2. Unemployment

The number of the registered unemployed topped half a million during 2005.[5] Official unemployment is thus very high and rising. The trend is particularly marked in the FBiH, where the ratio of the employed to jobseekers is down from 1.5 in 2001 to just 1.1 in 2005.[6] The situation in the RS is somewhat better, as the ratio has not changed significantly, around the 1.6 mark.

Gender analysis of unemployment in 2005 shows a ratio of 47 unemployed women to 53 men. This ratio is the same in both entities.[7]

The official unemployment data suggest a very alarming situation. Many experts hold that official unemployment is inflated, because of the large number of people in the informal economy and a number of quantitative analyses, based on different methodologies, present estimated 'real' unemployment rates, which we will not go into here. Such employment is certainly not sustainable or desirable in the long-term and the official data at very least make clear that this is a crucial and problematic area.

3. Inflation, the cost of living, and the CBBiH reserves

Retail prices and living costs rose moderately over the year. In the FBiH, prices rose on average 2.8 % against 2004, while living costs rose 2.7 %.[8] In the RS, retail prices rose 5.2%, while living costs rose 3.2 %.[12] It is worth noting that prices rose more in 2005 than in 2004.

2   The values of the indices were respectively: 198.6; 188.1; and 181.4. Source: RS Statistics Office, Statement of Industrial Statistics, No. XIV/1, January 2006.
3   Source: Federal Statistics Office, February 2006.
4   Source: RS Statistics Office, Statement of Industrial Statistics, No. XIV/1, January 2006.
5   Source: Table I in annex
6   Source: Table I in annex; author's calculations.
7   Source: Federal Employment Bureau, www.fzzz.ba; RS Employment Bureau.
8   Source: Federal Statistics Office, January 2006.
9   Source: RS Statistics Office, Saopštenje statistike cijena, no. XV/1, January 2006.

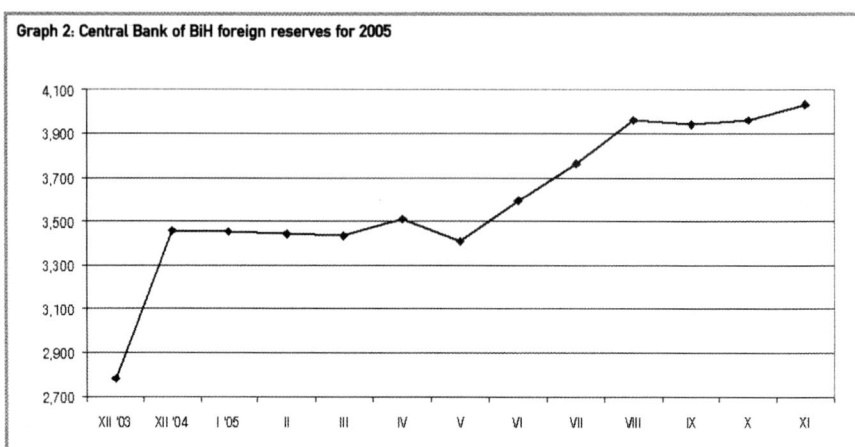

Graph 2: Central Bank of BiH foreign reserves for 2005

Source: CBBiH, Mjesečni bilansi stanja (privremeni). www.cbbh.gov.ba, February, 2006.

Central bank reserves have risen over recent years, despite the steadily rising trade deficit. During 2005, the foreign reserves rose from 3.5 billion KM to over 4 billion KM, or nearly 600 million KM. This is certainly a positive signal regarding the BiH economic environment and it is to be hoped that the trend will continue through 2006.

4. Foreign trade

BiH's foreign trade has for some years been marred by negative trends, a low import-export ratio and a rising deficit. The balance of trade showed some improvement between 2004 and 2005 in the import-export

Table II
Foreign Trade of BiH for 2000-2005

	EXPORTS	IMPORTS	VOLUME	BALANCE	RATIO
2000	1,969,682	7,114,154	9,083,836	-5,144,472	27.69
2001	1,806,725	6,563,599	8,370,324	-4,756,874	27.53
2002	1,888,321	6,881,311	8,769,632	-4,992,990	27.44
2003	2,313,211	8,274,741	10,587,952	-5,961,530	27.96
2004	2,994,219	9,371,258	12,365,477	-6,377,039	32.00
2005.	3,826,489	11,081,125	14,907,614	-7,254,636	34.50

Source: Foreign Trade Chamber of BiH, *Pregled ostvarene vanjskotrgovisnke razmjene za BiH za period I-XII 2004. i 2005. godine*, Sarajevo, January 2006

ratio. Exports were up 28% on the year before, but the data still clearly shows an import-dependent economy and a rising deficit.

The trade deficit reached 7.3 billion KM in 2005, the highest to date. The import-export ratio has been improving over the past two years, but the low initial value for exports and the high one for imports mean that it is growing in absolute terms. With official GDP for 2005 likely to top 13 billion KM, the trade deficit is more than 50% of GDP.

Most of the trade deficit is with EU members: 52% or 3.8 billion KM. The free trade agreement co-signatories take second place at 38%. Other trading partners account for the remaining 10%. For several 21 years, the main trade deficits have been with Croatia, Germany, Slovenia, Serbia and Montenegro, and Italy. In 2005, Croatia led at 1.7 billion KM, followed by Germany, at 867 million KM.[10]

The main importing sectors were machines, equipment, mechanical devices, boilers, vehicles, and weapons, and agricultural products and food and drinks. The main exporting sectors were ores, metals, and related products, and wood, paper, and furniture.[11]

5. The road to Europe

BiH's strategic goal is full and equal membership of the European Union. This is one of the few long-term goals about which there is general consensus here. So we must ask how close the country is to attaining its goal.

There are membership conditions which BiH must meet. They include the economic criteria set out in Copenhagen and Maastricht. Essentially, they relate to attaining adequate convergence with the level of development of EU countries. Without going into detailed analysis of the convergence criteria, we can compare BiH and EU countries on key economic indicators.

Table III
BiH and the EU (15), EU (25) - Key economic indicators

INDICATORS	EU (25)	BH
Real GDP growth, %	2.4	5.7
GDP per capita, EU 15 = 100, as % of EU 15	87.9	7.3
Unemployment, as % of labour force	8.0	43.2
Inflation rate (CPI), annual average	2.1	0.4
Budget deficit, as % GDP	- 2.6	- 0.1
Current account deficit, as % GDP	0.2	- 17.3
Public debt, as % GDP	63.8	59.7

Source: Eurostat, EC, ECB

We can see that BiH is not far behind the EU countries on inflation, budgetary deficit, and public debt. The position is critical, however, regarding industry. GDP per capita is only around 8 % of the EU 25 average, or 7.3 % of the EU 15. Official unemployment in BiH is so high that is not comparable to EU levels. Finally, the balance of payments, on which the international credibility of a country is built, is very bad. Our crude comparison suggests that the key economic challenges for BiH will be to increase *per capita* GDP, reduce unemployment, and correct external imbalances, i.e. the current account deficit. Significant progress in these areas certainly requires long-term commitment accompanied by long-term sustainable growth.

6. Public opinion

The public does not expect any major changes in the economic situation over the next year, or think that it changed much over the past one. In December, 36% of the sample thought that economic circumstances had worsened, which was the highest level all year. In fact, the numbers describing the situation as bad have been rising since the second quarter of 2005.

---

10 Source: Foreign Trade Chamber BiH, *Pregled ostvarene vanjskotrgovisnke razmjene za BiH za period I-XII 2004. i 2005*, Sarajevo, January 2006.

11 Imports for machines, equipment, and mechanical devices, boilers, vehicles, and weapons amounted to 2.95 billion KM, while agricultural and alimentary products amounted to 1.97 billion KM. Exports of ores, metals and related products amounted to 1.07 billion KM, while wood, paper, and furniture amounted to 679 million KM. Source: Foreign Trade Chamber BiH, *Pregled ostvarene vanjskotrgovisnke razmjene za BiH za period I-XII 2004. i 2005*, Sarajevo, January 2006.

ANNUAL REPORT 2005
A YEAR IN REVIEW

INCOME AND SOCIAL WELFARE

The Social Stability Index

A number of events combined to depress the Social Stability Index during 2005: strikes, protests, resignations, bankrupcies and closures. This resulted in more low income families, falling purchasing power and living standards, fear for the future, and increased readiness to protest.

Some indicators may suggest a society in hibernation (e.g. the inter-ethnic and the security stability indices), but the social and economic stability indices both fell to their lowest ever points during 2005. During the third quarter, it was as low as 42 points, to rise just one point by the end of the year.

This situation will certainly have repercussions for many areas of public life during the coming election year. Politicians will have to address it, if they wish to persuade voters that they can lead BiH out of the morass of the past several years. Success in social sector reform requires the energetic committment of all involved, not just superficial initiatives. The level of public scepticism hardly holds out much hope for sucessful implementation, however.

The backlog of social problems awaiting serious discussion (healthcare, education, social welfare) suggests that the country is still in the downward spiral of transition as regards socio-economic conditions. The public awaited the New Year in nervous anticipation of further privatization, general economic deterioration, and rising prices due to VAT introduction.

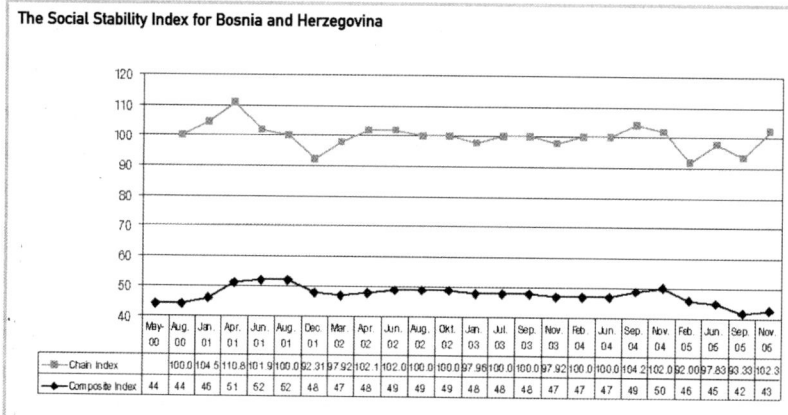

The Social Stability Index for Bosnia and Herzegovina

	May 00	Aug 00	Jan 01	Apr 01	Jun 01	Aug 01	Dec 01	Mar 02	Apr 02	Jun 02	Aug 02	Okt 02	Jan 03	Jul 03	Sep 03	Nov 03	Feb 04	Jun 04	Sep 04	Nov 04	Feb 05	Jun 05	Sep 05	Nov 05
Chain Index		100.0	104.5	110.8	101.9	100.0	92.31	97.92	102.1	102.0	100.0	100.0	97.96	100.0	100.0	97.92	100.0	100.0	104.2	102.0	92.00	97.83	93.33	102.3
Composite Index	44	44	46	51	52	52	48	47	48	49	49	48	48	48	47	47	47	49	50	46	45	42	43	

1. Household income

For most households, income levels in 2005 were similar to those in 2004. (See Tables I and II in annex). While there has been a minor improvement in extreme poverty, most households remain obviously unable to break out of the poverty trap and there has been a fairly significant increase in the number of low income households, particularly in Bosniak majority areas.

As Table I shows, there was a fall in 2005 in the number of households on less than 100 KM per month, but it actually affected only the FBiH (from 7.4% to 2.8%), and not the RS (up from 7% to 8.46%).

29

Table I
Monthly household income, including all wages and income of all household members, child allowance, pension and all other sources of income (in %)

	Nov 2004			Nov 2005		
	BiH	FbiH	RS	BiH	FbiH	RS
	%	%	%	%	%	%
No income	4.0	4.0	3.7	1.92	2.72	0.57
<100 KM/DM	7.6	7.4	7.0	5.11	2.80	8.46
101 - 200	11.8	11.0	12.6	15.59	15.74	15.23
201 - 300	15.0	15.5	13.8	14.18	11.87	16.50
301 - 400	11.0	10.2	12.6	12.26	11.51	13.96
401 - 500	10.3	7.1	15.6	13.03	13.73	11.75
501 - 600	5.9	5.8	6.3	6.33	6.11	6.94
601 - 700	5.1	4.1	6.7	4.62	4.93	4.11
701 - 800	3.4	4.0	2.4	3.83	4.14	3.54
801 - 900	4.3	5.1	3.4	2.48	2.75	2.17
901 - 1000	2.4	2.4	2.6	4.12	4.85	2.93
1001 - 1100	2.0	2.1	1.9	1.83	1.71	2.09
1101 - 1200	1.3	1.8	0.6	1.25	1.61	0.78
1201 - 1300	0.7	1.0	0.3	0.78	0.72	0.90
1301 - 1400	1.5	2.0	0.9	0.43	0.37	0.50
1401 - 1500	0.7	1.1	-	1.76	2.54	0.67
1501 - 1600	1.0	1.4	0.5	0.07	0.03	0.12
1601 - 1700	0.6	0.9	0.2	0.23	0.30	0.15
1701 - 1800	0.3	0.5		0.16	0.18	0.15
1801-1900						
1901 - 2000				0.49	0.46	0.57
> 2000 KM/DM	0.8	1.4		0.75	1.01	0.42
NA	10.2	11.3	9.0	8.79	9.92	7.49
TOTAL	100	100	100	100	100	100
No income	4.0	4.0	3.7	1.92	2.72	0.57
< 100 KM	7.6	7.4	7.0	5.11	2.80	8.46
101 - 200	11.8	11.0	12.6	15.59	15.74	15.23
201 - 300	15.0	15.5	13.8	14.18	11.87	16.50
301 - 400	11.0	10.2	12.6	12.26	11.51	13.96
401 - 500	10.3	7.1	15.6	13.03	13.73	11.75
SUBTOTAL to 500	59.70	55.20	65.30	62.09	58.37	66.48

Source: Opinion poll carried out for EWS by PRISM Research

In contrast, the percentage of the population reporting less than 500KM per month has actually risen, from 59.7% at the beginning to 62% at the end of the year.[1] Here, the rise is greater in the FBiH than in the RS (from 55.2% to 58.37% and from 65.3% to 66.48% respectively). This gives a somewhat false picture, however, as the differences between Bosniak and Croat majority areas in the FBiH are as great as those between the entities. In fact, the positions of Serbs and Bosniaks have converged over the year (Serbs from 62.8% to 66.5%, Bosniaks from 56.2% to 66.8%), so that now they appear almost equally impoverished. The number of low income Croat houses was relatively stable over the year and much lower, *at around* 28%. (See Table III).

As one might expect, the minority population is generally poorer than the majority one. The only exception is Bosniak majority areas in the final poll of the year. Equally interestingly and more reassuringly, the number of low income minority households in Croat and Bosniak majority areas actually fell during 2005 (from 52.28% to 33% and from 70.39% to 61.13%, respectively). The situation deteriorated in Serb majority areas (from 67.89% to 81.01%), however. (See Table III).

---

30   1   We focus on low income households (<500 KM) as the consumer basket cost on average 450 KM this year.

**UNHCR Representation
in Bosnia and Herzegovina**

UNHCR
The UN
Refugee Agency

Statistical Summary

as at 31 May 2006

I. Total Number of Refugees and Displaced Persons who Returned to/within Bosnia and Herzegovina*

	Total to date	Current year
A. Returns from Abroad	442,292	162
B. Returns of Displaced Persons	571,820	2,120
Total Number of Returnees :	1,014,112	2,282

II. Total Number of Minority Returns (Refugees and DPs) who Returned to their Place of Origin in BiH*

	Total to date	Current year
A. Federation of BiH	272,597	750
B. Republika Srpska	162,132	1,141
C. Brcko District	21,382	-
Total Number of Minority Returns :	456,111	1,891

* Since GFAP - General Framework Agreement for Peace in BiH

III. Refugees, Asylum Seekers and DPs in BiH

	Total	Federation	RS	Brcko District
A. Refugees :	10,494	3,064	7,397	33
From Croatia (Preliminary results)	7,382	-	7,349	33
From Serbia and Montenegro (Kosovo)	3,100	3,052	48	-
- in Collective Facilities	566	566	-	-
From Other Countries	12	12	-	-

	Total	Federation	RS	Brcko District
B. Asylum Seekers :	168	168	-	-
From Serbia and Montenegro (Incl. Kosovo)	107	107	-	-
- in Collective Accommodation (RCs)	74	74	-	-
From Other Countries	61	61	-	-
- in Collective Accommodation (RCs)	31	31	-	-

	Total	Federation	RS	Brcko District
C. Displaced Persons :	180,627	91,600	87,430	1,597
- DPs in Collective Centres	552	461	91	-

For the full UNHCR statistics package issued monthly please visit : *www.unhcr.ba*

Source: UNHCR; Municipal Authorities; DP Associations and NGOs

Given to the Author by UNCHR, Majda Prajlac.

144

Bosnia and Herzegovina/IDPs and Local Inhabitants/Gorazde Close-Ups
Watching the arrival of the first buses from Sarajevo; a symbol of resurrection after many months of suffering and isolation.
Photo: UNHCR/26012/03.1996/R.LeMoyne. Courtesy of Archives UEL, UK.

Bosnia and Herzegovina/IDPs/Boris Stankovic Primary School, Banja Luka/Shelter
This gymnasium turned collective centre houses more than 400 displaced persons. They are part of the estimated 120,000 who had to flee western Bosnia during the Croat recapture of the Krajina.
Photo: UNHCR/26226/05.1996/A.Hollmann. Courtesy of Archives UEL, UK.

Bosnia and Herzegovina/IDP. Displaced Persons/Hrasnica, Sarajevo/Shelter
Many of Sarajevo's buildings, like this collective centre housing IDPs, were badly damaged during the war. Repair and reconstruction must get underway as soon as possible in order to accommodate returnees.
Photo: UNHCR/25175/12.1995/L.Taylor. Courtesy of Archives UEL, UK.

Yugoslavia/Refugees from Bosnia Herzegovina/Sremska Mitrovica, Serbia/Arrival
The tractor which brought this man and his family to safety also became their temporary shelter.
Photo: UNHCR/22036/05.1992/A.Hollmann. Courtesy of Archives UEL, UK.

Index